© Assimil 2015
ISBN 978-2-7005-0652-5
ISSN 2266-1158

Graphic design: Atwazart

Spanish

Juan Córdoba & Belén Ausejo Aldazábal

Adapted for English speakers
by Paul Gerard Pickering

B.P. 25
94431 Chennevières sur Marne cedex
France

This phrasebook doesn't claim to be a substitute for a language course, but if you devote a bit of time to reading it and learning a few useful phrases, you'll quickly find that you're able to participate in basic exchanges with Spanish speakers, enriching your travel experience.

A word of advice: don't aim for perfection! Those you're speaking to will forgive any mistakes and appreciate your efforts to communicate in their language. The main thing is to leave your inhibitions behind and speak!

Section I

Section II

Section III

Section IV

Introduction

↗ **How to use this book**

Section 1: Getting started in Spanish

Can you spare a half an hour a day? Do you have three weeks ahead of you before your trip? In that case, jump in with the mini-lessons specially designed to familiarize you with Spanish in just 21 days. These mini-lessons are aimed at beginners with no prior knowledge of Spanish and will give you the basics you need to understand and address people in all sorts of situations.

• Discover the day's lesson, using the phonetic transcriptions to help you read the Spanish out loud. Repeat it as many times as you wish!

• Check the translation in everyday English, as well as the word-for-word translation, which will help you get used to the structure of the language.

• Read the notes that follow the lesson – these explain key linguistic points so you can apply them in other contexts.

• Finally, do the short exercise to consolidate what you've learned.

The next day, move on to the following lesson! Taking the time to do a little Spanish each day is the most effective way to learn and remember it.

Section 2: Conversing

This section gives you the tools you'll need for dealing with a variety of situations in which you might find yourself during your trip. It provides useful vocabulary and expressions that you can use in a range of contexts. The Spanish is accompanied by a translation, as well as a phonetic transcription that will help you pronounce it. This ready-to-use 'survival kit' is all you need to be an independent traveller!

↗ Spain: facts & figures

Surface area	505,370 km²
Population	47,737,000 inhabitants (July 2014 estimate)
Capital	Madrid
Territories	Balearic Islands, Canary Islands, 2 autonomous cities in Morocco (Ceuta and Melilla) and three small islands off the coast of Morocco
Land boundaries	France, Portugal, Andorra, Gibraltar (British Overseas Territory), Morocco
Sea boundaries	Bay of Biscay (Cantabrian Sea), Atlantic Ocean, Mediterranean Sea
Languages	Spanish (Castilian); regional languages including Galician, Basque, Catalan and Valencian
Government	Constitutional monarchy; Spain is made up of 17 autonomous regions, plus the two autonomous cities of Ceuta and Melilla on the Moroccan coast.
National holiday	12 October (commemorating the arrival of Christopher Columbus in the Americas)

Spain is the second-largest country in the European Union in area (after France). It is dominated by a high interior plateau surrounded on virtually all sides by mountain chains. The highest mainland peak is Mulhacén (3,478 m) in the Sierra Nevada, but the highest peak in all of Spain is Pico de Teide (3,710 m) on Tenerife in the Canary Islands. Apart from northern Spain, the climate is quite dry.

The 15th largest economy in the world, Spain has a large service sector, as well as sizeable industrial and agricultural sectors. In the decades following the 1980s, the country experienced a boom fuelled by real estate (**la burbuja inmobiliaria** *the real-estate bubble*). However, the 2008 financial crisis hit Spain hard, taking unemployment to record levels and ushering in a period of recession from which the country is slowly recovering.

The predominant religion in Spain is Roman Catholicism.

Spain is the third most-visited tourist destination in the world!

↗ **A bit of history**

711–1492: Seven centuries of Muslim presence

In 711, Muslim forces from North Africa invaded Spain and within seven years had conquered almost all of the Iberian Peninsula. Muslim-ruled Iberia was called **al-Andalus**, and its heartland was the region of southern Spain now known as Andalusia. Islamic Spain became one of the great Muslim civilizations, reaching its summit in the 900s. Over the centuries of Muslim rule, Christian kingdoms in the north fought to reconquer Spain, a period called the **Reconquista**. They finally succeeded in 1492, with the fall of Granada to the Catholic monarchs of Castile and Aragon.

Seven centuries of Muslim presence left their mark on Spanish culture and architecture, and on its landscape and language. As well as exceptional monuments such as the Great Mosque of Córdoba and the Alhambra Palace in Granada, Spanish has many words borrowed from Arabic: **azúcar** *sugar*, **arroz** *rice*, **aceite** *oil*, etc. The period was also a golden age of learning, with Muslim scholars bringing Greek philosophy and scientific knowledge (notably in medicine, physics and astronomy) to

Europe, translating the ancient Greek into Arabic, which was in turn translated into Latin by Spanish Christians.

1492–1800s: The Spanish Empire

Starting from 1492, the date Christopher Columbus arrived in the Caribbean, Spain took over territory that would make it a global empire that lasted for more than three centuries. At the height of its power, Spain ruled most of South and Central America as well as large territories in today's southwestern United States, and had possessions in Europe, Africa, the Atlantic and Pacific Oceans and the Far East.

1936–78: From dictatorship to democracy

In modern times, Spanish history was most marked by the Spanish Civil War (1936–39), started when General Francisco Franco led a coup against the republican government in a bid to restore more conservative rule. Backed by Fascist Italy and Nazi Germany, Franco's forces defeated the **Frente Popular** and he became the dictator of Spain from 1939 until his death in 1975. His repressive government banned opposition after a war that left many hundreds of thousands dead. After Franco's death, Spain returned to democracy with a constitutional monarchy, joining the European Union in 1986.

↗ **The Spanish language**

Spanish (**español**) is the native language of more than 400 million people, making it the second most-spoken language in the world. It is the official language in 21 countries and is also used daily by tens of millions of people in the United States. This phrasebook is intended for visitors to Spain, so it is based on Castilian Spanish (**castellano**); however, occasional differences with Latin American Spanish are pointed out.

The alphabet

The Spanish alphabet is almost the same as the English alphabet, apart from the letter **ñ**.

a *[ah]*, **b** *[bay]*, **c** *[thay]*, **d** *[day]*, **e** *[ay]*, **f** *[ayfay]*, **g** *[hay]*, **h** *[ahchay]*, **i** *[ee]*, **j** *[hotah]*, **k** *[kah]*, **l** *[aylay]*, **m** *[aymay]*, **n** *[aynay]*, **ñ** *[aynyay]*, **o** *[o]*, **p** *[pay]*, **q** *[koo]*, **r** *[ayray]*, **s** *[aysay]*, **t** *[tay]*, **u** *[oo]*, **v** *[oobay]*, **w** *[oobay doblay]*, **x** *[aykees]*, **y** *[ee gryaygah]*, **z** *[thaytah]*.

Pronunciation and accentuation

More good news is that Spanish pronunciation is phonetic, i.e. words are pronounced as they are spelled and virtually every letter is pronounced. However, it does include some sounds that don't exist in English. The phonetic transcriptions will help you pick up the right pronunciation –read them aloud with gusto and pretend you're Spanish!

Here are a few of the main pronunciation differences:
• **The rolled 'r'**: The Spanish **r** is made by lightly vibrating the tongue against the roof of the mouth. A single **r** is a short roll; when doubled or at the beginning of a word it is a longer roll.

- **The guttural 'j' and 'g':** The letter **g** (only when before **e** or **i**) and the letter **j** are a guttural *[h]* sound made at the back of the throat, as in the Scottish word *loch*: **gente** *[hayntay]* people.
- **The silent 'h':** The letter **h** is always silent (apart from in letter combinations such as **ch**): **hablar** *[ahblahr]* to talk.
- **The double 'll':** This is pronounced like the *[y]* in *yes*: **llamar** *[yahmahr]* to call.
- **The 'ñ':** This is a *[nyuh]* sound: **señor** *[senyor]* man, Mr.
- **The 'v':** This is a soft *[b]* sound: **vaca** *[bahka]* cow.
- **The Castilian 'lisp':** This total misnomer refers to the fact that the letter **c** (only before **e** or **i**) and the letter **z** are pronounced like the *[th]* in *think*: **zumo** *[thoomo]* juice; **cena** *[thaynah]* dinner.

Spanish accentuation (where the stress is placed in a word) is quite straightforward. Typically, the second-to-last syllable is emphasized: **patata** *potato*; **hombre** *man*. However, sometimes a different syllable is stressed. Rather than explain all the rules, we have just put the stressed syllable in bold in the phonetic transcriptions – you'll find you soon pick up the rhythm of the language. Note that if a vowel carries a written accent (**á**, **é**, **í**, **ó**, **ú**), this syllable should always be stressed.

So now you're ready to get started! **¡Buena suerte!** *Good luck!*

Getting started

↗ **Day 1**

¿Cómo te llamas?
What's your name?

1 **¡Hola! ¿Cómo te llamas?**

*olah **ko**mo tay **yah**mahs*

hello! how yourself *(informal)* you-call

Hello! What's your name?

2 **Me llamo Peter. Soy inglés.**

*may **yah**mo Peter soy een**glays***

myself I-call Peter. I-am English *(m.)*

My name is Peter. I'm English.

3 **Y tú, Mary, ¿de dónde eres?**

*ee too Mary day **don**day **ay**rays*

and you *(informal)* Mary from where you-are

And you, Mary, where are you from?

4 **Yo también soy inglesa.**

*yo tahm**byen** soy een**glay**sah*

I also I-am English *(f.)*

I'm English too.

Notes

Spanish has different ways of saying *you*. To address one person informally, you use **tú**. We'll see the other forms later.

Soy inglés(m.)/**inglesa**(f.). Spanish nouns are either masculine or feminine. Adjectives that describe a noun must agree with its

gender. So when referring to a male or female, a word may be a bit different. Here are the rules for saying where you are from:
• Nationalities ending in **-o** change to **-a** in the feminine form: **americano/americana** *American* (m./f.).
• If they end in a vowel other than **-o**, the masculine and feminine forms are the same: **canadiense** *Canadian*; **israelí** *Israeli* (m./f.).
• If they end in a consonant, an **-a** ending is added in the feminine and the accent is omitted: **escocés/escocesa** *Scottish* (m./f.).

Me llamo ('I call myself') is the equivalent of *My name is*. The verb **llamarse** includes a reflexive pronoun, indicating that the subject is performing the action on itself (e.g. *myself, yourself, himself, etc.*). Reflexive pronouns come <u>before</u> the verb.

ser *to be*		**llamarse** *to be called*	
(yo) soy	*I am*	**(yo) me llamo**	*I am called*
(tú) eres	*you* (inf.) *are*	**(tú) te llamas**	*you* (inf.) *are called*
(él/ella) es	*he/she/it is*	**(él/ella) se llama**	*he/she/it is called*

Practice—Translate the following sentences:
1. I am Canadian.
2. My name is Peter. I am English.
3. **¿De dónde es Mary?**
4. **¿Eres inglesa?**

Answers:
1. Soy canadiense.
2. Me llamo Peter, soy inglés.
3. Where is Mary from?
4. Are you *(f.)* English?

Presentaciones
Introductions

1 **¡Buenos días, Laura! ¿Cómo estás?**
   bwaynos deeahs laoorah komo estahs
   good days Laura! how you-are *(informal)*
   Good morning, Laura! How are you?

2 **¡Bien! Mira, te presento a una amiga australiana.**
   byen meerah tay praysento ah oonah ahmeegah aoostrahlyahnah
   well! look you *(informal)* I-present to a friend *(f.)* Australian
   Fine! Here, let me introduce an Australian friend to you.

3 **Encantado. Soy Rafa, un amigo de Laura.**
   enkahntahdo soy rrahfah oon ahmeego day laoorah
   enchanted. I-am Rafa a friend *(m.)* of Laura
   Nice to meet you. I'm Rafa, a friend of Laura's.

4 **Encantada. Soy Mary. Estoy de vacaciones en España.**
   enkahntahdah soy Mary estoy day bahkahthyonays en espahnyah
   enchanted. I-am Mary. I-am of vacations in Spain
   Nice to meet you. I'm Mary. I'm on holiday in Spain.

Notes
There are two verbs for *to be*: **ser** is used to describe unchanging characteristics (name, nationality, etc.) → **Soy Mary.** *I'm Mary.* **Soy inglesa.** *I'm English* (f.). The verb **estar** is used to describe temporary conditions (mood, health, location, etc.) → **¿Cómo estás?** *How are you?* Here are the conjugations in the singular: **(yo) estoy** *I am*; **(tú) estás** *you are* (inf.); **(él/ella) está** *he/she/it is*.

Note that subject pronouns (**yo** *I*, **tú** *you*, **él** *he*, **ella** *she*, etc.) are often left out, unless emphasis is needed: **Soy inglés, pero tú eres español.** *I am English, but <u>you</u> are Spanish*.

• Typically, a masculine noun or adjective ending in **-o** changes to **-a** in the feminine: **amigo → amiga**; **encantado → encantada**.
• The indefinite article *a/an* also has two forms: **un** (m.), **una** (f.).

Did you notice that exclamations and questions are punctuated on both sides in Spanish? → **¡Hola! ¿Cómo estás?**

Practice—Translate the following sentences:
1. Let me introduce an American friend *(m.)* to you.
2. Pleased *(f.)* to meet you. How are you?
3. Soy un amigo de Laura.
4. ¿Estás de vacaciones en España?

Answers:
1. Te presento a un amigo americano.
2. Encantada. ¿Cómo estás?
3. I'm a friend *(m.)* of Laura's.
4. Are you on holiday in Spain?

⟋ **Day 3**

Familia y trabajo
Family and work

1 **¿Cuántos años tienes?**
   kwahntos ahnyos tyenes
   how-many years you-have *(informal)*
   How old are you ?

2 **Tengo cuarenta y cinco años.**
   tengo kwahrentah ee theenko ahnyos
   I-have forty and five years
   I'm forty-five.

3 **Tengo dos hijos y dos hijas.**
   tengo dos eehos ee dos eehahs
   I-have two sons and two daughters
   I have two sons and two daughters.

4 **¿En qué trabajas?**
   en kay trahbahhahs
   in what you-work *(informal)*
   What do you do?

5 **Trabajo en una agencia de viajes.**
   trahbahho en oonah ahhenthyah day byahhays
   I-work in an agency of travels
   I work in a travel agency.

Notes

There are three verb groups, which conjugate in slightly different ways: verbs ending in **-ar**, **-er** or **-ir**. Let's look at the singular conjugations of two common verbs: **trabajar** to work (which is a regular **-ar** verb) and **tener** to have (an irregular **-er** verb).

(yo) trabajo	I work	**(yo) tengo**	I have
(tú) trabajas	you (informal) work	**(tú) tienes**	you (informal) have
(él/ella) trabaja	he/she works	**(él/ella) tiene**	he/she/it has

To form the plural of a noun ending in a vowel, just add an **-s**: **un hijo y una hija** a son and a daughter → **dos hijos y dos hijas** two sons and two daughters. (Note that **hijos** can mean either sons or children, i.e. sons and daughters.)

We've already seen some useful words for asking questions: **¿Cómo?** How? **¿Dónde?** Where? **¿De dónde?** From where? **¿Qué?** What? **¿En qué?** In what? In line 1, we see **¿Cuánto?** How much? **¿Cuántos?** How many? When used with a noun, it has to agree in gender and number: **¿Cuántas amigas?** How many friends (f.)? But with a verb, the form is always masculine singular: **¿Cuánto cuesta?** How much does that cost?

Practice – Translate the following sentences:
1. Where do you work?
2. How many children do you have?
3. **Trabajo en Inglaterra.**
4. **Tengo una hija y dos hijos.**

Answers:
1. **¿Dónde trabajas?**
2. **¿Cuántos hijos tienes?**
3. I work in England.
4. I have one daughter and two sons.

↗ Day 4

Por favor...
Please ...

1 **Perdón, no hablo bien español. ¿Habla usted inglés?**
*payr**don** no **ah**blo byen espah**nyol** ah**blah** oo**ste**ᵈ een**glays***
pardon not I-speak well Spanish. speak you *(formal)* English
Sorry, I don't speak Spanish well. Do you speak English?

2 **No, lo siento. ¿Le puedo ayudar en algo?**
*no lo **syen**to lay **pway**do ahyoo**dar** en **ahl**go*
no it I-regret. you *(formal)* I-can help in something
No, I'm sorry. Can I help you with anything?

3 **Sí, por favor. ¿Está lejos de aquí la Plaza Mayor?**
*see por fah**bor** es**tah** **lay**hos day ah**kee** lah **plah**thah mah**yor***
yes for favour. it-is far from here the square main
Yes, please. Is the main square far from here?

4 **¡Está muy cerca! Le acompaño.**
*es**tah** **moo**ee **thayr**kah lay ahkom**pah**nyo*
it-is very near! you *(formal)* I-accompany
It's very close! I'll go with you.

Notes

Two very useful words: **sí** *yes* and **no** *no*. To form a negative sentence, just put **no** before the verb: **no hablo** *I do not speak*.

To address someone very politely, for example, an older stranger or superior, the formal *you* is used: **usted**. The verb conjugates in the third-person singular in this case. → **¿Habla (usted) inglés?** *Do you speak English?*

There are also formal and informal object pronouns (pronouns that receive the action of the verb). *I'll go with you* in the informal is **te acompaño** ('I accompany you'), whereas in the formal it is **le acompaño** (**le** is one of the third-person object pronouns).

Unlike in English, note that object pronouns usually come <u>before</u> the verb: **¿Le puedo ayudar?** *Can I help you* (formal)? And adjectives usually come <u>after</u> the noun: **una amiga irlandesa** *an Irish friend;* **la plaza mayor** *the main square.*

Practice—Translate the following sentences:
1. Are you *(f.) (formal)* English?
2. I'm *(m.)* English. I don't speak Spanish very well.
3. ¿Le puedo hablar en inglés?
4. Lo siento, no le puedo acompañar.

Answers:
1. ¿Es usted inglesa?
2. Soy inglés. No hablo español muy bien.
3. Can I speak to you *(formal)* in English?
4. I'm sorry, I can't go with you *(formal)*.

De tapas
Going out for tapas

1 **¿Quieres jamón serrano, tortilla…?**

*kyayrays hah**mon** sayrrahno tor**teey**ah*

you-want *(informal)* ham [of] mountain, omelette

Do you want cured ham [or maybe] Spanish omelette…?

2 **Aquí la tortilla está muy buena, las albóndigas también.**

*ah**kee** lah tor**teey**ah es**tah moo**ee **bway**nah lahs ahl**bon**deegahs
tahm**byen***

here the omelette is very good, the meatballs too

The tortilla is very good here; the meatballs, too.

3 **Me gusta más el pescado.**

*may **goos**tah mahs el pes**kah**do*

to-me it-appeals more the fish

I prefer fish.

4 **¿Te gustan los calamares?**

*tay **goos**tahn los kahlah**mah**rays*

to-you *(informal)* they-appeal the squids

Do you like squid?

5 **¡Sí, me encantan! ¡Quiero calamares!**

*see may en**kahn**tahn **kyay**ro kahlah**mah**rays*

yes me they-enchant! I-want squids

Yes, I love it! I want squid!

Notes

There are four forms for *the* in Spanish: **el** (m. sing.), **la** (f. sing.),
los (m. plural), **las** (f. plural). When talking about something

generally, the definite article is used: **Me gusta el pescado**. *I like fish.* **¿Te gustan los calamares?** *Do you like squid?*

To form the plural of a noun ending in a consonant, you add **-es**: **el calamar → los calamares**.

querer means *to want* (**quiero tapas** *I want tapas*), but also *to love* in the romantic sense (**te quiero** *I love you*). Here are the singular forms: **(yo) quiero, (tú) quieres, (él/ella/usted) quiere**.

To say that you like something, you use **me gusta** ('to-me it-appeals') for something singular or **me gustan** ('to-me they-appeal') for something plural. If you <u>really</u> like something, you can use **me encanta** or **me encantan**, which is formed in the same way. **¡Me encanta la tortilla!** *I love Spanish omelette!*

Practice—Translate the following sentences:
1. Do you *(formal)* want the fish?
2. I don't like squid.
3. Me encantan las albóndigas.
4. ¿Te gusta la tortilla?

Answers:
1. ¿Quiere usted pescado?
2. No me gustan los calamares.
3. I love meatballs.
4. Do you *(informal)* like Spanish omelette?

↗ **Day 6**

¿Te gusta España?
Do you like Spain?

1 **¿Eres de aquí o estás de vacaciones?**
ayrays day ahkee o estahs day bahkahthyonays
you-are *(informal)* from here or you-are of vacations
Are you from here or are you on holiday?

2 **No, no soy de aquí; vivo en Inglaterra, en Londres.**
no no soy day ahkee beebo en eenglahtayrrah en londrays
no not I-am of here; I-live in England in London
No, I'm not from here; I live in England, in London.

3 **Estamos aquí de vacaciones, mi familia y yo.**
estahmos ahkee day bahkahthyonays mee fahmeelyah ee yo
we-are here of vacations my family and I
My family and I are here on vacation.

4 **Venimos a España todos los años.**
bayneemos ah espahnyah todos los ahnyos
we-come to Spain all the years
We come to Spain every year.

5 **Nos gusta mucho España. Hablamos español.**
nos goostah moocho espahnyah ahblahmos espahnyol
to-us it-appeals much Spain. we-speak Spanish
We like Spain a lot. We speak Spanish.

Notes

The use of prepositions can vary from one language to another. The preposition in a certain context might not always be the one you expect! Some common prepositions include **a** *to, at;* **en** *in, on*; **de** *of, from*. But in Spanish it is **de vacaciones** <u>*on*</u> *holiday* and **¿Le puedo ayudar en algo?** *Can I help you* <u>*with*</u> *something?*

In line 5, we see a new object pronoun: **nos gusta España** ('Spain appeals to <u>us</u>') *we like Spain.*

Here are the present tense conjugations of regular verbs ending in **-ar** and in **-ir**, and of the irregular verbs **estar** and **venir**.

Subject pronouns	Verbs			
	hablar *to speak*	vivir *to live*	estar *to be*	venir *to come*
yo *I*	hablo	vivo	estoy	vengo
tú *you* (inf. sing.)	hablas	vives	estás	vienes
él/ella *he/she/it* **usted** *you* (formal sing.)	habla	vive	está	viene
nosotros/-as *we*	hablamos	vivimos	estamos	venimos
vosotros/-as *you* (inf. pl.)	habláis	vivís	estáis	venís
ellos/ellas *they* (m./f.) **ustedes** *you* (formal pl.)	hablan	viven	están	vienen

Practice—Translate the following sentences:
1. We don't live in London.
2. We like to come on holiday to Spain.
3. No soy de aquí.
4. Están aquí.

Answers:
1. No vivimos en Londres.
2. Nos gusta venir de vacaciones a España.
3. I'm not from here.
4. They are here.

↗ **Day 7**

El mercado del pueblo
The town market

1 **Esta mañana vamos al mercado del pueblo.**
estah mahnyahnah bahmos ahl mayrkahdo del pwayblo
this morning we-go to-the market of-the town
This morning we're going to the town market.

2 **Me encanta este mercado.**
may enkahntah estay mayrkahdo
me it-enchants this market
I love this market.

3 **Hola, guapa. ¿Qué vas a querer?**
olah gwahpah kay bahs ah kayrayr
hello beautiful. what you-are-going to want
Hello, love. What would you like?

4 **¿A cuánto están estas uvas?**
ah kwahnto estahn estahs oobahs
at how-much are these grapes
How much are these grapes?

5 **Y estos plátanos, ¿qué precio tienen?**
ee estos plahtahnos kay praythyo tyenen
and these bananas what price they-have
And these bananas, how much are they?

Notes

The words for *this* and *these*, referring to something close (in space or time) are: **este** (m. sing.), **esta** (f. sing.), **estos** (m. plural),

estas (f. plural). They need to agree with the noun they are used with: **este pueblo** *this town*; **estas uvas** *these grapes*.

The masculine singular definite article **el** *the* contracts with certain prepositions: **a + el = al** *to the*; **de + el = del** *of the*. **Voy al mercado del pueblo.** *I'm going to the market of the town*.

ir *to go* is frequently followed by **a** *to*: **Voy al mercado.** *I'm going to the market*. This verb is often used to express something that will take place in the near future: **voy a tener** *I'm going to have*. You'll notice that sometimes where English uses the present continuous (*to be + -ing*), Spanish uses the simple present tense: **¿Vienes?** *Are you coming?* The conjugation of **ir** is: **(yo) voy, (tú) vas, (él/ella/usted) va, (nosotros) vamos, (vosotros) vais, (ellos/ellas/ustedes) van**.

Practice—Translate the following sentences:
1. How much is this fish?
2. This banana isn't very good.
3. **Nos encanta este pueblo.**
4. **Voy al mercado, ¿vienes?**

Answers:
1. **¿A cuánto está este pescado?**
2. **Este plátano no está muy bueno.**
3. We love this town.
4. I'm going to the market, are you *(informal)* coming?

↗ Day 8

¿Vamos a la playa?
Are we going to the beach?

1 ¿Quién viene a la playa conmigo?
  kyen byaynay ah lah plahyah konmeego
  who comes to the beach with-me
  Who's coming to the beach with me?

2 No puedo, lo siento.
  no pwaydo lo syento
  not I-can it I-regret
  I can't, I'm sorry.

3 A ver, ¿por qué no puedes?
  ah bayr por kay no pwaydays
  to see for what not you-can *(informal)*
  Well, why can't you?

4 ¡Porque tengo que trabajar!
  porkay tengo kay trahbahhahr
  because I-have that work
  Because I have to work!

5 También hay que descansar un poco, ¿no?
  tahmbyen I kay deskahnsahr oon poko no
  also there-is that to-rest a bit, no
  One has to rest a bit too, right?

Notes

tener que + infinitive expresses *to have to do something*. Just conjugate **tener** in the appropriate person: **tengo que trabajar**

I have to work, **tienes que trabajar** *you have to work,* etc. Another way of expressing obligation (without saying who is obligated) is **hay que** + infinitive *to be necessary to*: **Hay que ir al mercado.** *It is necessary to go to the market.* (or more idiomatically in English *We/I/You have to go to the market.*) (Note that **hay** on its own means *there is/are*: a very useful word!)

Some verbs have a spelling change in the stem when conjugated in certain persons and tenses. Two common stem-changing verbs are **querer** *to want, to love* → **(yo) quiero, (tú) quieres,** etc. and **poder** *to be able to (can)* → **(yo) puedo, (tú) puedes, (él/ella/usted) puede, (nosotros) podemos, (vosotros) podéis, (ellos/ellas/ustedes) pueden**.

Two more useful question words: **¿Quién?** *Who?* and **¿Por qué?** *Why?* In the plural, **¿Quién?** becomes **¿Quiénes?**: **¿Quiénes son?** *Who are they?* Also note that while **¿Por qué?** *Why?* is two separate words, the reply **porque** *because* is a single word.

Practice—Translate the following sentences:
1. It is necessary to go to the market.
2. Who wants to come with me?
3. ¿Por qué no vienes a la playa?
4. No podemos porque tenemos que trabajar.

Answers:
1. Hay que ir al mercado.
2. ¿Quién quiere venir conmigo?
3. Why don't you *(informal)* come to the beach?
4. We can't because we have to work.

↗ Day 9

Tomar café
Having a coffee

1 **¿Qué van a tomar ustedes?**
*kay bahn ah to**mahr** oo**ste**^days*
what are-you-going to take you *(formal plural)*
What are you going to have?

2 **Yo voy a tomar un café con leche, pero con poca leche.**
*yo boy ah to**mahr** oon kah**fay** kon **lay**chay **pay**ro kon **po**kah
laychay*
I am-going to take a coffee with milk but with little milk
I'll have a coffee with milk, but with just a little milk.

3 **¿Y para usted, caballero?**
*ee **pah**rah oo**ste**^d kahbah**yay**ro*
and for you *(formal sing.)* sir
And for you, sir?

4 **Para mí lo contrario: un café con mucha leche.**
***pah**rah mee lo kon**trah**ryo oon kah**fay** kon **moo**chah **lay**chay*
for me the opposite: a coffee with much milk
For me, the opposite: a coffee with a lot of milk.

5 **¿Quieren algo para acompañar los cafés?**
kyay**ren **ahl**go **pa**rah ahkompah**nyahr** los kah**fays
you-want *(formal plural)* something for to-accompany the coffees
Do you want something to go with the coffees?

Notes

In the context of eating or drinking, **tomar** *to take* is used rather than *to have*: **tomar el desayuno** *to have breakfast*.

The preposition **para** *for, to, in order to* is often used to indicate purpose or final objective → **para usted** *for you*.

To politely address more than one person, **ustedes** *you* (pl.) is used with the third-person plural verb: **¿Qué quieren ustedes, señores?** *What do you want, gentlemen?* The respectful forms of address **señor/caballero** *sir* and **señora** *madam* are still common in Spain.

poco *a little* and **mucho** *a lot* can be used with a verb (**Duermo mucho.** *I sleep a lot.*) or with a noun, in which case they need to agree in gender and number: **poca leche** (f.) *little milk*, **muchos pueblos** *many towns*, etc.

Practice—Translate the following sentences:
1. What are you *(formal pl.)* going to have, gentlemen?
2. For me a coffee, and for him a coffee with milk.
3. Yo quiero mucha leche y poco café.
4. ¿Quiere usted algo para acompañar el café?

Answers:
1. ¿Qué toman ustedes, señores?
2. Para mí un café y para él un café con leche.
3. I want a lot of milk and not much coffee.
4. Do you *(formal sing.)* want anything to go with the coffee?

No estoy bien
I'm not well

1 **Creo que estoy enfermo, doctor.**
  *kray*o kay es**toy** en**fayr**mo dok**tor**
  I-believe that I-am ill *(m.)* doctor
  I think that I'm ill, doctor.

2 **¿Le duele algo?**
  lay **dway**lay **ahl**go
  to-you *(formal)* pains something
  Does anything hurt?

3 **Me duele la cabeza, me duelen las piernas...**
  may **dway**lay lah kah**bay**thah *may* **dway**len lahs **pyayr**nahs
  to-me pains the head, to-me pain the legs
  My head hurts, my legs hurt ...

4 **Es un resfriado.**
  *es oon rraysfree**ah**do*
  it-is a cold
  It's a cold.

5 **Le voy a recetar estas pastillas y este jarabe.**
  *lay boy ah rraythay**tahr** es*tahs pahs**tee**yahs ee *es*tay hah**rah**bay
  to-you *(formal)* I-am-going to prescribe these pills and this syrup
  I'm going to prescribe these pills and this cough syrup for you.

Notes

Remember that **ser** is used to describe essential characteristics:
Es galés. *He is Welsh.* **Es alta.** *She is tall.* It is also used before a

noun: **Es un resfriado.** *It's a cold.* To describe a temporary state (mood, health, etc.), use **estar: estoy contento/-a** *I'm happy* (m./f.), **está enfermo/-a** *he/she is ill.*

To say that something hurts, use **me duele** ('to-me it-pains') for one thing or **me duelen** ('to-me they-pain') for more than one thing. If someone else is hurting, just change the object pronoun: **Le duelen las piernas.** *His/Her/Your* (formal) *legs hurt.* Note that whereas English uses a possessive adjective (*my, your, his, her,* etc.) to refer to a body part, Spanish uses a definite article.

As we've seen, formal address uses the third person. So the object pronoun **le** can mean *he, she, it* or *you* (formal). **¿Le gusta España?** *Does he/she like Spain?* or *Do you like Spain?*

Practice—Translate the following sentences:
1. You are ill, sir; you have a cold.
2. Do your *(formal)* legs hurt?
3. **Te voy a recetar un jarabe.**
4. **No me gusta tomar pastillas.**

Answers:
1. **Está usted enfermo, señor, tiene un resfriado.**
2. **¿Le duelen las piernas?**
3. I'm going to prescribe a cough syrup for you *(informal)*.
4. I don't like to take pills.

⌐ **Day 11**

Buscando un regalo
Looking for a present

1 **Estoy buscando un regalo para mi novia.**
   *es**toy** boos**kahn**do oon rraygahlo **pah**rah mee **no**byah*
   I-am looking-for a present for my girlfriend
   I'm looking for a present for my girlfriend.

2 **¿Cómo es tu chica?**
   ***ko**mo es too **chee**kah*
   how she-is your *(informal)* girl
   What is your girlfriend like?

3 **Es clásica con su familia y moderna cuando sale con sus amigas.**
   *es **klah**seekah kon soo fah**mee**lyah ee mo**dayr**nah **kwahn**do **sah**lay kon soos ah**mee**gahs*
   she-is traditional with her family and modern when she goes-out with her friends
   She's traditional with her family and modern when she goes out with her friends.

4 **¿Por qué no le compras un abanico?**
   *por kay no lay **kom**prahs oon ahbah**nee**ko*
   why not for-her you-buy a fan
   Why don't you buy her a fan?

Notes

To talk about an action in progress, a conjugated form of **estar** + present participle is used. This is called the progressive tense and generally corresponds to *to be + -ing*: **estoy buscando** *I am looking for* (at this very moment). However, we've seen that the simple present is sometimes used to convey this meaning as well: **¿Qué buscas?** *What are you looking for?*

The present participle is formed by replacing an **-ar** infinitive ending with **-ando**, or an **-er** or **-ir** infinitive ending with **-iendo**: **Estamos comiendo.** *We are eating.*

The words to show possession (by one person) are **mi** *my*, **tu** *your* (informal), **su** *his/her/your* (formal). An important difference from English is that if what is possessed is plural, an **-s** needs to be added: **mis amigas; tus hijos; sus hijas.**

If **cuando** *when* is used as a question word, a written accent is added: **¿Cuándo vienes?** *When are you coming?* (The same is true for **¿Qué?, ¿Dónde?, ¿Quién?** and other question words.)

Practice—Translate the following sentences:
1. I'm going to have a coffee with my friends.
2. When are you *(informal)* going to come?
3. ¿Dónde estás? ¡Tu novio te está buscando!
4. Le estoy comprando un regalo.

Answers:
1. Voy a tomar un café con mis amigos.
2. ¿Cuándo vas a venir?
3. Where are you *(informal)*? Your boyfriend is looking for you.
4. I am buying him a present.

⌐ Day 12

En la zapatería
At the shoe shop

1 **¿Puede enseñarme algunos modelos de zapatos de vestir?**

*pway*day ensay*nyar*may ah*lgoo*nos mo*day*los day thah*pah*tos day bes*teer*

you-can *(formal)* show-me some models of shoes of dressing

Can you show me some styles of dress shoes?

2 **¿Cuál es su talla?**

*kwahl es soo tah*ya

which is your *(formal)* size

What is your size?

3 **Estos zapatos me gustan bastante pero me aprietan demasiado.**

*es*tos thah*pah*tos may *goo*stahn bah*stahn*tay *pay*ro may ah*pryay*tahn daymah*syah*do

these shoes to-me they-appeal rather but me they-squeeze too-much

I rather like these shoes, but they are too tight.

4 **Estos son menos bonitos pero más cómodos.**

*es*tos son *may*nos bo*nee*tos *pay*ro mahs *ko*modos

these are less pretty but more comfortable

These are not as nice but are more comfortable.

Notes

Although object pronouns generally come before the verb, with an infinitive there are two options: before the conjugated verb or attached to the end of the infinitive. **¿Me puede enseñar?** or **¿Puede enseñarme?** *Can you show me?*

Since formal address is in the third person, the possessive *your* (formal) is **su**: **¿Cuál es su talla?** *What is your size?*

Adjectives not only have to agree with a noun's gender, but also its number (singular or plural): **Estos zapatos no son cómodos.** *These shoes are not comfortable.*

Here are some useful words for making comparisons: **más** *more*; **menos** *less*; **demasiado** *too much*; **bastante** *rather, enough*. When used with a noun, the last two need to agree: **No hay bastantes tallas.** *There aren't enough sizes.* **Hay demasiadas albóndigas.** *There are too many meatballs.*

Practice—Translate the following sentences:
1. I have to buy myself some shoes.
2. Your *(formal)* shoes are very pretty.
3. Hay que trabajar más.
4. Compro demasiados zapatos.

Answers:
1. Tengo que comprarme zapatos. / Me tengo que comprar zapatos.
2. Sus zapatos son muy bonitos.
3. I/You/We have to work more.
4. I buy too many shoes.

↗ **Day 13**

Al salir del cine
Leaving the cinema

1   **¿Te ha gustado la película?**
tay ah goostahdo lah payleekoolah
to-you *(informal sing.)* it-has appealed the film
Did you like the film?

2   **Más o menos. Me ha parecido un poco larga.**
mahs o maynos may ah pahraytheedo oon poko lahrgah
more or less. to-me it-has seemed a bit long
More or less. It seemed a bit long.

3   **A mí me ha encantado.**
ah mee may ah enkahntahdo
to me to-me it-has enchanted
I loved it.

4   **Y a vosotros, ¿os ha gustado?**
ee ah bosotros os ah goostahdo
and to you *(informal plural)* to-you it-has appealed
How about you, did you like it?

5   **¡Nos ha parecido muy larga y aburridísima!**
nos ah pahraytheedo mooee lahrgah ee ahboorreedeeseemah
to-us it-has seemed very long and very-boring
We thought it was very long and very boring!

Notes

To talk about a recent action in the past, the present perfect is used. It is formed with the conjugated auxiliary verb **haber** *to have* (**he, has, ha, hemos, habéis, han**) + past participle. This is formed by replacing an **-ar** infinitive ending with **-ado**, or an **-er** or **-ir** infinitive ending with **-ido**: **he hablado** *I have spoken*; **has comido** *you have eaten*; **ha venido** *he/she has come*, etc.

When talking to more than one person informally, **vosotros/-as** *(m./f.)* is the subject pronoun and **os** is the object pronoun. The corresponding present tense verb ends in **-áis, -éis** or **-ís**.

The full set of indirect object pronouns (*to me, to you*, etc.) are **me, te, le, nos, os, les**: e.g. **les ha parecido** *it seemed to them*.

After a preposition, the subject pronouns are used, except for **mí** and **ti**: **para mí** *for me*; **a ti** *to you*; **con vosotros** *with you* (pl.).

Either **muy** *very* or the suffix **-ísimo/-a** can be used to emphasize an adjective: **muy aburrida = aburridísima** *very boring*.

Practice—Translate the following sentences:
1. They loved the film.
2. I didn't like your *(informal sing.)* friends.
3. **¿Habéis ido al cine?**
4. **Sandra me ha hablado de ti.**

Answers:
1. **Les ha encantado la película.**
2. **No me han gustado tus amigos.**
3. Did you *(informal plural)* go to the cinema?
4. Sandra has spoken to me about you.

↗ Day 14

Horarios
Schedules

1 ¿A qué hora cenáis en España?
*ah kay **o**rah thay**nah**ees en es**pah**nyah*
at what hour you-dine *(informal plural)* in Spain
What time do you have dinner in Spain?

2 Aquí se cena a partir de las diez.
*ah**kee** say **thay**nah ah pahr**teer** day lahs dyayth*
here one dines at parting of the ten
Here people have dinner from ten o'clock on.

3 Y nos levantamos a las siete más o menos.
*ee nos laybahn**tah**mos ah lahs **syay**tay mahs o **may**nos*
and us we-raise at the seven more or less
And we get up at around seven o'clock.

4 ¡Vuestras noches son más cortas que las nuestras!
*bway**strahs no**chays son mahs **kor**tahs kay lahs **nway**strahs*
your *(informal plural)* nights are more short than the ours
Your nights are shorter than ours!

Notes

A little review of the regular **-ar**, **-er** and **-ir** conjugations:

yo		cen**o**		com**o**		viv**o**
tú		cen**as**		com**es**		viv**es**
él/ella/usted	cenar *to dine*	cen**a**	comer *to eat*	com**e**	vivir *to live*	viv**e**
nosotros/-as		cen**amos**		com**emos**		viv**imos**
vosotros/-as		cen**áis**		com**éis**		viv**ís**
ellos/ellas/ustedes		cen**an**		com**en**		viv**en**

In reflexive verbs, the pronoun is essential to the meaning: it cannot be left out. It is placed before the verb: **levantarse** *to get up* ('to raise oneself') → **me levanto, te levantas, se levanta, nos levantamos, os levantáis, se levantan.**

The reflexive pronoun **se** can convey 'one', i.e. 'people in general': **Se vive bien en España.** *One lives well in Spain.*

The words to show possession (by more than one person) are **nuestro/-a** *our*, **vuestro/-a** *your* (informal), **su** *their/your* (formal). The first two need to agree in gender with the noun they precede. For all three, if what is possessed is plural, an **-s** is added: **nuestras amigas; vuestros hijos; sus hijas.**

Practice—Translate the following sentences:
1. Our Spanish friends get up at seven.
2. You *(informal plural)* can come with all your friends.
3. Si quiere, puede venir a cenar.
4. Aquí se habla inglés.

Answers:
1. Nuestros amigos españoles se levantan a las siete.
2. Podéis venir con todos vuestros amigos.
3. If you *(formal sing.)* wish, you can come and have dinner.
4. English is spoken here.

↗ Day 15

En la estación
At the station

1 **¿Puede decirme dónde está la estación, por favor?**
pwayday daytheermay donday estah lah estahthyon por fahbor
can-you *(formal)* tell-me where is the station for favour
Can you tell me where the station is, please?

2 **Quisiera un billete para Londres.**
keesyayrah oon beeyaytay pahrah londrays
I-would-like a ticket for London
I'd like a ticket to London.

3 **¿Sería tan amable de darme un asiento al lado de la ventanilla?**
sayreeah tahn ahmahblay day dahrmay oon ahsyaynto ahl lahdo day lah bentahneeyah
would-you-be *(formal)* so kind of give-me a seat at-the side of the window
Would you be so kind as to give me a window seat?

4 **Desearía también un billete de vuelta.**
daysayahreeah tahmbyen oon beeyaytay day bwayltah
I-would-desire also a ticket of return
I would also like a return ticket.

5 **¿Puedo pagarle con tarjeta?**
pwaydo pahgahrlay kon tahrhaytah
can-I pay-to-you *(formal)* with card
Can I pay with a credit card?

The conditional can be used to make a statement more polite, e.g. *I would like*. In Spanish, the conditional is formed by adding an ending to the infinitive: **ser** *to be* → **sería** *I would be*, **serías** *you (inf. sing.) would be*, **sería** *he/she/it/you (for. sing.) would be*, **seríamos** *we would be*, **seríais** *you (inf. pl.) would be*, **serían** *they/ you (for. pl.) would be*.

However, for **querer** *to want, to like*, a verb form called the imperfect subjunctive is used rather than the conditional to mean *would like*. As it's such a useful verb in the context of asking for something politely, it's a good idea to know these forms: **quisiera, quisieras, quisiera, quisiéramos, quisierais, quisieran.**

Practice—Translate the following sentences:
1. Can you *(formal sing.)* speak to me in English?
2. I would like to pay with a credit card.
3. Desearía un asiento al lado de la ventanilla, por favor.
4. ¿Sería tan amable de decirme dónde está la estación?

Answers:
1. ¿Puede hablarme en inglés?
2. Quisiera pagar con tarjeta.
3. I would like a window seat, please.
4. Would you be so kind as to tell me where the station is?

↗ **Day 16**

¿Dónde vamos a dormir?
Where are we going to sleep?

1   **¿Sabría decirme si hay un hotel barato por aquí?**
*sah**bree**ah day**theer**may see I oon o**tel** bah**rah**to por ah**kee***
would-you-know *(formal)* to-tell-me if there-is a hotel cheap by here
Could you tell me if there is a cheap hotel around here?

2   **Le aconsejaría buscar en otro barrio: este es bastante caro.**
*lay ahkonsayhah**reee**ah boo**skar** en **o**tro **bah**rryo **es**tay es bah**stahn**tay **kah**ro*
to-you *(formal)* I-would-advise to-search in other neighbourhood: this-one is rather expensive
I would advise you to search in another neighbourhood; this one is rather expensive.

3   **¿Tendría habitaciones libres?**
*ten**dree**ah ahbeetah**thyon**ays **lee**brays*
would-you-have *(formal)* rooms free
Do you have any rooms available?

4   **¿Me podría decir cuál es el precio por noche?**
*may po**dree**ah day**theer** kwahl es el **pray**thyo por **no**chay*
to-me could-you *(formal)* tell what is the price per night
Could you tell me what the price per night is?

Notes

Here are some useful verbs that are irregular in the conditional (the stem changes slightly): **poder** → **podría usted** *could you*; **tener** → **tendría usted** *would you have*; **saber** → **sabría usted** *would you know*. (In line 1, this verb is used in the sense of 'to know how', which is similar to **podría** *you could*.)

Those tricky prepositions again: **por noche** *per night*, but **por aquí** *around here*, **por correo** *by post* and **por la mañana** *in the morning*. Over time you'll get used to which to use when!

otro/-a *other, another* (never preceded by **un** or **una**): **otro hotel** *another hotel*, **otra noche** *another night*.

Practice—Translate the following sentences:
1. Could you *(formal)* speak to me in English?
2. Would you *(formal)* have a room for three nights?
3. ¿Sabría decirme cuánto cuesta un billete para Nueva York?
4. Quisiera una habitación para mí y otra para mi hija.

Answers:
1. ¿Podría hablarme en inglés?
2. ¿Tendría una habitación para tres noches?
3. Could you tell me how much a ticket to New York costs?
4. I would like a room for me and another for my daughter.

⤴ **Day 17**

¿Quedamos?
Shall we meet?

1 **Dime cuándo quedamos para salir de copas.**
   *deemay **kwahn**do kay**dah**mos **pah**rah sah**leer** day **ko**pahs*
   tell-me *(informal)* when we-stay for to-go-out for glasses
   Tell me when we're meeting to go out for a drink.

2 **No lo sé todavía. Dame tu número de móvil y te llamo.**
   *no lo say todah**bee**ah **dah**may too **noo**mayro day **mo**beel ee tay*
   *yah*mo
   not it I-know yet. give-me *(informal)* your number of mobile and you I-call
   I don't know yet. Give me your mobile number and I'll call you.

3 **Llámame mañana por la mañana entonces.**
   *yah*mahmay mah**nyah**nah por lah mah**nyah**nah en**ton**thays*
   call-me *(informal)* tomorrow around the morning then
   Call me tomorrow morning then.

4 **Si no contesto, deja un mensaje.**
   *see no kon**tes**to **day**hah oon men**sah**hay*
   if not I-answer leave *(informal)* a message
   If I don't answer, leave a message.

Notes

An imperative verb is used to give an order or make a request.
When speaking to one person informally, use the '**tú**' imperative
(just drop the final **-s** of the second-person singular present):
hablas *you speak* → **¡Habla!** *Speak!* or **comes** *you eat* → **¡Come!**
Eat! Line 1 has an irregular verb: **decir** *to say, to tell* → **dices** *you*
say/tell → **¡Di!** *Say! Tell!*

If an object pronoun is used with an imperative, it is attached at the end (in some cases a written accent has to be added): **¡Llámame!** *Call me!* **¡Dinos!** *Tell us!* **¡Enséñale!** *Show him!*

Some useful points:
• The word **todavía** can mean *yet* or *still.*
• The first-person singular of **saber** *to know* is **sé** *I know.*
• **mañana** means both *tomorrow* and *morning*, and the phrase **mañana por la mañana** means *tomorrow morning.*
• Don't confuse **sí** *yes* and **si** *if!*

Practice—Translate the following sentences:
1. Shall we meet in the morning to have a coffee?
2. I don't know yet if I'm going to be able to go out tomorrow.
3. **Llámame y dime dónde quedamos.**
4. **Déjame tu número de móvil.**

Answers:
1. **¿Quedamos por la mañana para tomar un café?**
2. **No sé todavía si voy a poder salir mañana.**
3. Call me and tell me where we're meeting.
4. Leave me your mobile number.

↗ **Day 18**

La invitación
The invitation

1 Ven a cenar mañana a casa con tu mujer.
*ben ah thay**nar** mah**nyah**nah ah **kah**sah kon too moo**hayr***
come *(informal)* to dine tomorrow at house with your wife
Come have dinner tomorrow at our house with your wife.

2 A Laura le encantaría conoceros.
*ah **la**oorah lay enkahntah**ree**ah kono**thayr**os*
to Laura to-her it-would-enchant to-meet-you *(informal pl.)*
Laura would be delighted to meet you.

3 Le he hablado mucho de vosotros.
*lay ay ah**blah**do **moo**cho day bo**so**tros*
to-her I-have spoken much of you *(informal pl.)*
I have spoken to her a lot about you.

4 Ten, Laura: Paco me ha dicho que te gustan las flores.
*ten **la**oorah **pah**ko may ah **dee**cho kay tay **goo**stahn lahs **flo**rays*
have *(inf.)* Laura: Paco to-me has said that to-you they-appeal the flowers
Here, Laura – Paco has told me that you like flowers.

5 Ponte cómodo: estás en tu casa.
***pon**tay **ko**modo e**stahs** en too **kah**sah*
put-yourself *(inf. sing.)* comfortable: you-are in your house
Make yourself comfortable, you are at home here.

Notes

The models for the regular **'tú'** informal imperative are **¡Habla!**
Speak! (verbs ending in **-ar**); **¡Come!** *Eat!* (verbs ending in **-er**) and

¡**Vive!** *Live!* (verbs ending in **-ir**). A few irregular verbs that don't follow this model are ¡**Di!** *Tell!* ¡**Ven!** *Come!* ¡**Ten!** *Have!* (in the sense of *Here you are!*), ¡**Pon!** *Put!* (in line 5, this is the reflexive verb **ponerse** with the meaning *to stand, to sit*).

We've already seen how to form regular past participles, e.g. **hablado** (see lesson 13), but there are a number that are irregular. Here are a few common ones: **dicho** *said, told*; **visto** *seen*; **puesto** *put*; **hecho** *done, made*.

Practice—Translate the following sentences:
1. Have you *(informal)* seen? They have eaten very little.
2. It's because you *(informal)* have made squid!
3. ¡Te he dicho que no les gustan los calamares!
4. Ponte aquí, al lado de Paco.

Answers:
1. ¿Has visto? Han comido muy poco.
2. ¡Es porque has hecho calamares!
3. I told you *(informal)* that they don't like squid!
4. Stand/Sit *(informal)* here, next to Paco.

⬈ **Day 19**

Por teléfono
On the telephone

1 Está hablando con nuestro contestador, espere un momento.
*es**tah** ah**blahn**do kon **nways**tro kontestah**dor** es**pay**ray oon mo**men**to*
you-are (*formal*) speaking with our answering-machine, wait a moment
You have reached our answering machine: wait one moment.

2 ¿Oiga? ¿Reservas?
*o**i**gah rray**sayr**bahs*
you-hear? (*formal*) reservations?
Hello? Reservations?

3 Para información diga "uno".
*pah**rah een**for**mah**thyon dee**gah **oo**no*
for information say (*formal*) one
For information, say 'one'.

4 ¡Póngame con reservas!
*pon**gahmay kon rray**sayr**bahs*
put (*formal*) me with reservations
Put me through to reservations!

5 Nuestros operadores están ocupados, llame más tarde.
*nways**trohs opayrah**dor**ays es**tahn okoo**pah**dos **yah**may mahs **tahr**day*
our operators are occupied, call (*formal*) more late
Our operators are busy, call back later.

Notes

When giving an order or making a request in the formal singular, use the '**usted**' imperative (for regular verbs, just change the final vowel of the '**tú**' imperative):

• **a → e** for **-ar** verbs: **¡Espera!** (inf.) → **¡Espere!** (formal) *Wait!*
• **e → a** for **-er** and **-ir** verbs: **¡Come!** (inf.) → **¡Coma!** (form.) *Eat!*
¡Vive! (inf.) → **¡Viva!** (form.) *Live!*

However, if a verb is irregular in the first-person singular present, the same irregularity is found in the '**usted**' imperative: **oigo** *I hear* → **¡Oiga!** *Listen!* (**oír** *to hear*); **digo** *I say* → **¡Diga!** *Say!* (**decir** *to say*); **pongo** *I put* → **¡Ponga!** *Put!* (**poner** *to put*), etc.

Hello? when answering the phone is **¡Diga!** or **¡Dígame!** ('*Tell me!*'). If you didn't catch something, you can say **¿Oiga?** *Excuse me?* Another use of **poner** is *to put through*: **póngame con Señora Lopez** *put me through to Ms Lopez.*

The equivalent of *-er* or *-est* is conveyed with **más** *more*: **más tarde** *later*; **más bonito** *prettier*; **el más barato** *the cheapest.*

Practice—Translate the following sentences:
1. Wait *(formal)* one moment.
2. Put *(formal)* me through to reservations, please.
3. Información, dígame, ¿en qué puedo ayudarle?
4. ¿Puede llamar más tarde?

Answers:
1. Espere un momento.
2. Póngame con reservas, por favor.
3. Information: Hello, how may I help you *(formal)*?
4. Can you *(formal)* call back later?

↗ **Day 20**

Por teléfono (sigue)
On the telephone (continued)

1 **Sí, dime.**
   *see **dee**may*
   yes tell-me *(informal)*
   Yes, hello?

2 **¡Hace una hora que te estoy llamando!**
   ***ah**thay **oo**nah **o**rah kay tay es**toy** yah**mahn**do*
   it-makes an hour that you *(informal)* I-am calling
   I've been calling you for an hour!

3 **Perdona y no grites, ¿vale? No he tenido cobertura.**
   *payr**do**nah ee no **gree**tays **bah**lay no ay ten**ee**do kobayr**too**rah*
   pardon and not shout *(informal)* it's-worth? not I-have had coverage
   Sorry and don't shout, OK? I didn't have coverage.

4 **¡No olvides comprar el pan!**
   *no ol**bee**days kom**prahr** el pan*
   not forget *(informal)* to-buy the bread
   Don't forget to buy the bread!

5 **Vale, ¡ponme con Antonio!**
   ***bah**lay **pon**may kon an**to**nyo*
   it's-worth, put-me *(informal)* with Antonio
   OK, let me speak to Antonio!

Notes

In this phone conversation, a couple addresses each other informally, so the person picking up says **¡Dime!** *Hello?* ('Tell me!').

In the same way, **¡Oiga!** would be **¡Oye!** *Hey! Excuse me!* and **póngame con** becomes **ponme con** *let me speak to.*

To say <u>not</u> to do something (the negative imperative) informally, it's **no** + the second-person singular of the subjunctive, i.e.:
• **-es** for **-ar** verbs: **¡No grit<u>es</u>!** *Don't shout!* (**gritar** *to shout*)
• **-as** for **-er** and **-ir** verbs: **¡No com<u>as</u>!** *Don't eat!* (**comer** *to eat*)
But if a verb is irregular in the first-person singular present, the same irregularity is found in the imperative: **¡No digas!** *Don't tell!*

hace ('it makes') is used to describe how long something has gone on. With the past tense, it translates to *ago*: **Te he llamado hace diez minutos.** *I called you ten minutes ago.*

Practice—Translate the following sentences:
1. Don't call *(informal)* me when I'm working, OK?
2. Sorry, but I forgot something.
3. ¡Dime! ¿Qué quieres? ¡Hace cinco minutos que me has llamado!
4. No compres el pan y ponme con Antonio, por favor.

Answers:
1. No me !lames cuando estoy trabajando, ¿vale?
2. Perdona, pero he olvidado algo.
3. Hello! What do you *(inf.)* want? You called me five minutes ago.
4. Don't buy *(inf.)* the bread and let me speak to Antonio, please.

↗ **Day 21**

En la calle
In the street

1 Perdone. ¿Podría decirme dónde queda el museo?

payrdonay podreeah daytheermay donday kaydah el moosayo

pardon could-you *(formal)* tell-me where stays the museum

Excuse me. Could you tell me where the museum is?

2 ¡Está bastante lejos de aquí!

estah bahstahntay layhos day ahkee

it-is rather far from here

It's quite a long way from here!

3 ¿Ve usted aquel edificio?

bay oostedᵈ ahkel edeefeethyo

see you *(formal)* that building

Do you see that building?

4 Vaya hasta allí, gire a la derecha y siga todo recto.

bahyah ahstah ahyee heeray ah lah dayraychah ee seegah todo rrekto

go *(formal)* until there, turn to the right and continue all straight

Go down there, turn to the right and keep going straight.

Notes

In formal address, use **perdone** instead of **perdona** (informal) (from **perdonar** *to pardon*). Two new irregular formal commands are **¡Vaya!** *Go!* (from **ir**) and **¡Siga!** *Continue!* (from **seguir**).

The words for *that* and *those*, referring to something distant (in space or time) are shown in the following table along with their counterparts for *this* and *these*.

	Near (**aquí** *here*)	Distant (**allí, allá** *there, over there*)
(m.)	**este museo** *this museum* **estos edificios** *these buildings*	**aquel museo** *that museum* **aquellos edificios** *those buildings*
(f.)	**esta calle** *this street* **estas casas** *these houses*	**aquella calle** *that street* **aquellas casas** *those houses*

And finally, some useful words for understanding directions: **cerca** *near*; **lejos** *far*; **hasta** *until*; **todo recto** *straight (on)*; **a la izquierda** *on the left*; **a la derecha** *on the right*.

Practice — Translate the following sentences:
1. Go *(formal)* down there, turn left and continue straight on.
2. It's too far!
3. Perdone, ¿podría decirme si hay una estación de metro cerca de aquí?
4. ¿Ve usted aquella casa, allí?

Answers:
1. Vaya hasta allí, gire a la izquierda y siga todo recto.
2. ¡Está demasiado lejos!
3. Excuse me *(formal)*, could you tell me if there is a metro station near here?
4. Do you *(formal)* see that house over there?

Conversing

↗ First contact

Aside from quite formal situations, Spaniards (especially young people) tend to use informal address, even with strangers. They are talkative and outgoing and often speak loudly.

Greetings

To decide which greeting is most appropriate for a certain time of day, you need to know the following: **la tarde** *(afternoon)* begins after lunch and continues until sunset, which means that **buenas tardes** can be heard until well into the evening. After dark, **la noche** *(night)* begins, so **buenas noches** is used not only as the greeting *good evening*, but also when saying *goodnight*.

Good morning!	¡Buenos días!	*bwaynos deeahs*
Good afternoon/ evening!	¡Buenas tardes!	*bwaynahs tahrdays*
Good evening/night!	¡Buenas noches!	*bwaynahs nochays*

These can be intensified or shortened.

Standard	Intensified	Abbreviated
¡Hola! *(Hello)*	*	*
¡Hola, buenos días!	¡Muy buenos días!	*
¡Hola, buenas tardes!	¡Muy buenas tardes!	¡Buenas! or ¡Muy buenas! (understood: tardes or noches)
¡Hola, buenas noches!	¡Muy buenas noches!	

Among friends, a mere handshake may seem a little cold. It is more usual to accompany it with a pat on the shoulder. Generally, people do not hesitate to give a hug (**el abrazo**) and a few friendly pats (**las palmadas**) on the back. Cheek kissing (**el beso**) is common for greeting women: one kiss on each cheek.

Saying goodbye

See you later!	¡Hasta luego!	*ah*stah **lway**go
See you!	¡Nos vemos!	*nos **bay**mos*
See you soon!	¡Hasta pronto!	*ah*stah **pronto**
See you tomorrow!	¡Hasta mañana!	*ah*stah **mahnyah**nah
Goodbye! / Bye!	¡Adiós!	*ah**dyos***

Addressing someone

sir / gentlemen	señor / señores	*say**nyor**/-ays*
madam / ladies	señora / señoras	*say**nyor**ah/-ahs*
miss / ladies	señorita / señoritas	*saynyo**reet**ah/-ahs*

Note that these forms of address are all used with much more frequency than their English counterparts.

don *[don]* or **doña** *[donya]* can be used with a first name as a sign of respect, for example, with older people: **Don Andrés, Doña María.**

Often, terms of endearment are added to friendly greetings and goodbyes: **¡Hola, guapa!** *Hello, beautiful!* **¡Hasta luego, niño!** *See you later, kid!*

Offering wishes

La bienvenida *welcome* is expressed using an adjective that agrees in gender and number with the person welcomed.

¡Bienvenido(s)! *(m.)*	*byenbay**nee**do(s)*
¡Bienvenida(s)! *(f.)*	*byenbay**nee**dah(s)*

When drinking, eating or travelling:

Cheers!	**¡Salud!**	*sah**loo**ᵈ*
Enjoy your meal!	**¡Buen provecho!** **¡Que aproveche!**	*bwayn pro**bay**cho* *kay ahpro**bay**chay*
Have a good trip!	**¡Buen viaje!**	*bwayn **byah**hay*

Agreeing and disagreeing

Yes.	**Sí.**	*see*
Of course.	**Claro.** **Claro que sí.** **Por supuesto.**	***klah**ro* ***klah**ro kay see* *por soo**pwes**to*
Okay.	**De acuerdo.** **Vale.**	*day ah**kwayr**do* ***bah**lay*
No.	**No.**	*no*
I'm sorry.	**Lo siento.**	*lo **syen**to*
Absolutely not.	**En absoluto.**	*en abso**loo**to*
Certainly not.	**Claro que no.** **Por supuesto que no.**	***klah**ro kay no* *por soo**pwes**to kay no*

Asking questions

When? ¿Cuándo?

When do you (formal) *open?*
¿Cuándo abre usted?
kwahndo ahbray oosted

I open at five.
Abro a las cinco.
ahbro ah lahs theenko

Where? ¿Dónde? / ¿Adónde? (with movement towards)

Where do you (formal) *live?*
¿Dónde vive usted?
donday beebay oosted

I live in ...	Vivo en...	beebo en
London.	Londres.	londrays
New York.	Nueva York.	nwaybah yor*

Where are you (inf.) *going?*
¿Adónde vas?
ahdonday bahs

I'm going to Spain.
Voy a España.
boy ah espahnyah

How? ¿Cómo?

How are you (inf.)*?*
¿Cómo estás?
komo estahs

I'm fine.
Estoy bien.
estoy byen

Why? / Because ¿Por qué? / Porque

Why are you (inf.) *leaving?*
¿Por qué te vas?
por kay tay bahs

Because I'm in a hurry.
Porque tengo prisa.
porkay tengo preesah

Who? ¿Quién?

Who is the last person in line?
¿Quién es el último?
kyen es el **ool**teemo

I am.
Soy yo.
soy yo

How much? ¿Cuánto?

How much does it cost?
¿Cuánto cuesta?
kwahnto **kwes**tah

Thanking someone

Thank you.	**Gracias.**	**grah**thyahs
Many thanks.	**Muchas gracias.**	**moo**chahs **grah**thyahs
Don't mention it.	**De nada.**	day **nah**dah
You're welcome.	**No hay de qué.**	no I day kay

Making yourself understood

Do you (formal) *speak English?*
¿Habla usted inglés?
ahblah oo**ste**ᵈ een**glays**

I don't understand.
No entiendo.
no en**tyen**do

Can you (formal) ...	¿Puede usted...	**pway**day oo**ste**ᵈ
repeat that?	**repetir?**	rraypay**teer**
speak more slowly?	**hablar más despacio?**	ah**blahr** mahs day**spah**thyo
spell the word?	**deletrear la palabra?**	daylaytray**ahr** lah pah**lah**brah

What does ... mean?
¿Qué quiere decir...?   or
kay **kyay**ray day**theer**

¿Qué significa...?
kay seegnee**fee**kah

↗ **Meeting people**

Running into someone

If the person is clearly older than you, use formal address (**usted, ustedes**). Otherwise, informal address (**tú, vosotros/-as**) is more frequent, although not in every situation. One tip is to start with a phrase that doesn't include the word *you*, and then wait to see how the other person addresses you!

Hello, how are you?	Hola, ¿qué tal?	*olah kay tahl*
Fine.	**Bien.**	*byen*
Great.	**Muy bien.**	*mooee byen*
Fantastic.	**Divinamente.**	*deebeenahmentay*
	Estupendamente.	*estoopendahmentay*
Not too bad.	**Así así.**	*ahsee ahsee*
	Regular.	*rraygoolahr*
Getting along.	**Tirando.**	*teerahndo*
Not too good.	**Mal.**	*mahl*
Really bad.	**Muy mal.**	*mooee mahl*
Awful.	**Fatal.**	*fahtahl*

Someone may suggest that you use informal address:

Let's use 'tú', okay?
Vamos a tutearnos, ¿te parece?
bahmos ah tootayahrnos tay pahraythay

Please don't use 'usted'!
¡No me trates de usted, por favor!
no may trahtays day oosteᵈ por fahbor

Here are the informal and formal versions to ask how someone is:

How are you? (inf.)	¿Cómo estás?	komo estahs
How are you? (formal)	¿Cómo está usted?	komo estah oosteᵈ
Fine, and you? (inf./form.)	Bien, ¿y tú?/¿y usted?	byen ee too / ee oosteᵈ

To show your pleasure at bumping into someone, you can also use the expression **¡Dichosos los ojos!** ('Happy the eyes!').

Introducing yourself or someone else

The Spanish have double surnames (**los apellidos**): traditionally, the father's surname comes first, followed by the mother's. The first name (**el nombre**) is often made into a diminutive by adding **-ito** or **-ita** (**Miguel → Miguelito, Ana → Anita**). Sometimes the diminutive is quite different: **José → Pepe, Francisco → Paco** or **Curro, Carmen → Carmela, Dolores → Lola**, etc.

| What's your name? | ¿Cómo te llamas? | komo tay yahmahs |
| What's your name? (formal) | ¿Cómo se llama usted? | komo say yahmah oosteᵈ |

| My name is ... | Me llamo... | may yahmo |
| This is ... (informal) | Te presento a... | tay praysento ah |

| Delighted. (m./f.) | Encantado/-a. | enkahntahdo/-ah |
| It's a pleasure. | Tanto gusto. | tahnto goosto |

Hello, how are things? My name is Juan.
Hola, ¿qué hay? Soy Juan.
olah kay I soy hwahn

Nice to meet you, I'm Luisa.
Encantada, yo soy Luisa.
enkahn**tah**dah yo soy l**wee**sah

It's a pleasure.
Tanto gusto.
tahnto **goo**sto

This is my friend Rafa. (informal)
Te presento a mi amigo Rafa.
tay pray**sen**to ah mee ah**mee**go **rrah**fah

Do you (informal) *know Laura? She's my girlfriend.*
¿Conoces a Laura? Es mi novia.
ko**no**thays ah **la**oorah es mee **no**byah

Saying where you're from

Where are you (informal) *from?*
¿De dónde eres?
day **don**day **ay**res

Where are you (formal) *from?*
¿De dónde es usted?
day **don**day es oo**ste**ᵈ

I am ... (m./f.)	Soy...	soy
American.	americano/-a.	ahmayree**kah**no/-ah
Australian.	australiano/-a.	aoostrah**lyah**no/-ah
British.	británico/-a.	bree**tah**neeko/-ah
Canadian.	canadiense.	kahnah**dyen**say
French.	francés / francesa.	frahn**thays**/-ah
German.	alemán / alemana.	ahlay**mahn**/-ah
Irish.	irlandés / irlandesa.	eerlahn**days**/-ah
New Zealander.	neozelandés / neozelandesa.	nayothaylahn**days**/-ah
South African.	sudafricano/-a.	soodafree**kah**no/-ah

Or you can specify that you're *English* (**inglés/inglesa**), *Scottish* (**escocés/escocesa**), *Welsh* (**galés/galesa**), *Indian* (**indio/-a**), etc.

You might also want to give some general information:

Where do you (informal) *live?*
¿Dónde vives?
*don*day *bee*bays

Where do you (formal) *live?*
¿Dónde vive usted?
*don*day *bee*bay oo**ste**ᵈ

I live in ...	Vivo en...	**bee**bo en
a medium-sized town.	**una ciudad mediana.**	**oo**nah thyoo**dah**ᵈ may**dyah**nah
a village.	**un pueblo.**	oon **pway**blo
the outskirts of ...	**las afueras de...**	lahs ah**fway**rahs day

Giving your age

For the numbers in Spanish, refer to the cover flaps. Be careful with 21, 31, 41, etc.: before the word **años, uno** becomes **un**.

How old are you? (informal)	**¿Qué edad tienes?** **¿Cuántos años tienes?**	kay ay**dah**ᵈ **tyen**ays **kwahn**tos **ahn**yos **tyen**ays
How old are you? (formal)	**¿Qué edad tiene usted?** **¿Cuántos años tiene usted?**	kay ay**dah**ᵈ **tyen**ay oo**ste**ᵈ **kwahn**tos **ahn**yos **tyen**ay oo**ste**ᵈ
I'm thirty-one.	**Tengo treinta y un años.**	**teng**o tray**een**tah ee oon **ahn**yos
I was born in 1980.	**Nací en 1980.**	nah**thee** en meel no**bay**-**thyen**tos o**chen**tah

Talking about your family

Family values remain strong in Spain. It is not uncommon, for example, for several generations to live under the same roof. This having been said, the revolution in mores of the post-Franco era has profoundly shaken up traditional lifestyles.

To talk about your family situation:

I am ... (m./f.)	Estoy...	estoy
married.	casado/-a.	kahsahdo/-ah
single.	soltero/-a.	soltayro/-ah
divorced.	divorciado/-a.	deeborthyahdo/-ah

I'm a widower / widow.	Soy viudo/-a.	soy byoodo/-ah

I have children.	Tengo hijos.	tengo eehos
We don't have any children.	No tenemos hijos.	no tenaymos eehos
We have two daughters and one son.	Tenemos dos hijas y un hijo.	tenaymos dos eehahs ee oon eeho

A distinction is made between *immediate family* (**la familia**) and *in-laws* (**la familia política**).

family	familia (f.)	fahmeelyah
parents	padres (m.)	pahdrays
father / mother	padre / madre	pahdray / mahdray
brother / sister	hermano/-a	ayrmahno/-ah
uncle / aunt	tío/-a	teeo/-ah
nephew / niece	sobrino/-a	sobreeno/-ah
cousin	primo/-a	preemo/-ah
grandparents	abuelos (m.)	ahbwaylos
grandfather/-mother	abuelo/-a	ahbwaylo/-ah
grandson/-daughter	nieto/-a	nyayto/-ah

in-laws	familia política (f.)	fahmeelyah poleeteekah
brother-/sister-in-law	cuñado/-a	koonyahdo/-ah

| son-/daughter-in-law | yerno / nuera | *yayrno / nwayrah* |
| father-/mother-in-law | suegro/-a | *swaygro/-ah* |

Saying what you do

So you've met someone and talked about where you're from and your family – the next subject is likely to be what you do.

What do you (informal) do?
¿A qué te dedicas?
ah kay tay daydeekahs

What do you (formal) do?
¿A qué se dedica usted?
ah kay say daydeekah ooste^d

What's your (informal) job?
¿En qué trabajas?
en kay trahbahhahs

What's your (formal) job?
¿En qué trabaja usted?
en kay trahbahhah ooste^d

In Spanish, when saying what you do, there is no *a/an* before the profession. There is often a masculine and feminine form.

I am (a/an) ... (m./f.)	Soy...	*soy*
business owner.	empresario/-a.	*empraysahryo/-ah*
civil servant.	funcionario/-a.	*foonthyonahryo/-ah*
employee.	empleado/-a.	*emplayahdo/-ah*
farmer.	agricultor/-a.	*ahgreekooltor/-ah*
labourer.	obrero/-a.	*obrayro/-ah*
manager.	ejecutivo/-a.	*ayhaykooteebo/-ah*
self-employed.	autónomo/-a.	*aootonomo/-ah*

When talking about a field of work, *the* is often needed.

I work in ...	Trabajo en...	*trahbahho en*
business.	el comercio.	*el komayrthyo*

construction.	la construcción.	*lah konstrook***thyon**
education.	la enseñanza.	*lah ensay***nyahn**thah
research.	investigación. *(f.)*	*eenbesteegah***thyon**

Or perhaps you're a student:
Are you (informal) *a student or are you working?*

¿Estudias o trabajas?

*es**too**dyahs o trah**bah**hahs*

I'm in lower secondary school. (age 12–16)	Estoy haciendo la ESO.	*es***toy** *ah***thyen**do lah **ay**so
I'm in upper secondary school. (age 16–18)	Estoy haciendo bachillerato.	*es***toy** *ah***thyen**do bahcheeyay**rah**to
I'm at university.	Estoy estudiando la carrera.	*es***toy** *estoo***dyahn**do lah kah**rray**rah

With or without a good degree, finding a job is no easy task, and the subject is a big topic of conversation among young Spaniards.

The National Employment Institute
El INEM (Instituo Nacional de Empleo) *[el* ***ee**nem]*

I am ...	Estoy...	*es***toy**
doing an internship ...	haciendo prácticas ...	*ah***thyen**do **prahk**teekahs
... with a company.	... en una empresa.	*en* **oo**nah em**pray**sah
taking a training course.	haciendo un cursillo.	*ah***thyen**do oon koor**see**yo
unemployed.	en el paro.	*en el* **pah**ro

Religion and traditions

Until 1978, Roman Catholicism was Spain's official religion and it remains predominant. Although today less than 15% of believers declare themselves practising churchgoers, Spanish culture is imbued with Catholic traditions: the most common first names are still **María** and **José** (*Mary* and *Joseph*), and the feast day of a person's patron saint (**el santo**) is celebrated just as much as their birthday.

Are you (informal) *religious?*
¿Eres creyente?
ayrays kray**yen**tay

Are you (formal) *religious?*
¿Es usted creyente?
es ooste^d kray**yen**tay

Yes, I believe in God.	**Sí, creo en Dios.**	see **kray**o en dyos
No, I don't believe in God.	**No, no creo en Dios.**	no no **kray**o en dyos
I believe in God, but I don't go to church.	**Soy creyente pero no soy practicante.**	soy kray**yen**tay **pay**ro no soy prahktee**kahn**tay

I go regularly …	**Suelo ir...**	**sway**lo eer
to church. (Catholic)	**a la iglesia.**	ah la ee**glay**syah
to church. (Protestant)	**al templo.**	ahl **templo**
to mass.	**a misa.**	ah **mee**sah
to pray.	**a rezar.**	ah rray**thahr**
to the mosque.	**a la mezquita.**	ah lah meth**kee**tah
to the synagogue.	**a la sinagoga.**	ah la seenah**go**gah

There is no *a/an* before giving your religion or beliefs.

I am (a/an) … (m./f.)	**Soy...**	soy
agnostic.	**agnóstico/-a.**	ahg**nos**teeko/-ah
atheist.	**ateo/-a.**	ah**tay**o/-ah
Buddhist.	**budista.**	boo**dee**stah
Catholic.	**católico/-a.**	kah**to**leeko/-ah

Evangelical.	evangelista.	aybahnhay**lee**stah
Jewish.	judío/-a.	hoo**dee**o/-ah
Muslim.	musulmán / musulmana.	moosool**mahn** / moosool**mah**nah
Orthodox.	ortodoxo/-a.	orto**dokso**/-ah
Protestant.	protestante.	protes**tahn**tay

The weather

In Spain, as in many countries, the weather is a popular subject! Careful: in Spanish you say what the weather <u>does</u> (**hacer**), not what it <u>is</u> (**estar**).

What's the weather going to be like tomorrow?
¿Qué tiempo va a hacer mañana?
*kay **tyem**po bah ah ah**thayr** mah**nyah**nah*

It's going to be ...	Va a hacer...	bah ah ah**thayr**
nice.	buen tiempo.	bwayn **tyem**po
hot.	calor.	kah**lor**
very hot.	mucho calor.	**moo**cho kah**lor**
cold.	frío.	**free**o
very cold.	mucho frío.	**moo**cho **free**o
bad weather.	mal tiempo.	mahl **tyem**po

It's going to ...	Va a...	bah a
rain.	llover.	yo**bayr**
snow.	nevar.	nay**bahr**
be windy.	hacer viento.	ah**thayr** **byen**to
be cloudy.	estar nublado.	es**tahr** noo**blah**do

Expressing opinions and likes/dislikes

Do you (informal) *like to dance?*
¿Te gusta bailar?
tay goostah bilar

Yes, I love it!
Sí, ¡me encanta!
see may enkahntah

So do I!
¡A mí también!
ah mee tahmbyen

No, I don't like it.
No, no me gusta.
no no may goostah

Neither do I.
A mí tampoco.
ah mee tahmpoko

What did you think of the film?	¿Qué te ha parecido la película?	kay tay ah pahraytheedo lah payleekoolah
I loved it.	Me ha encantado.	may ah enkahntahdo
I thought it was very funny.	Me ha parecido divertidísima.	may ah pahraytheedo deebayrteedeeseemah
I didn't like it at all.	No me ha gustado nada.	no may ah goostahdo nahdah

If a more detailed opinion is required, you can add:

I think that ...	Pienso que...	pyenso kay
I believe that ...	Creo que...	krayo kay
I suppose that ...	Supongo que...	soopongo kay
I hate ...	Me horroriza...	may orroreethah
I have the feeling that ...	Tengo la sensación de que...	tengo lah sensahthyon day kay

Accepting invitations

Much of the social life in Spain takes place out of the home: people meet friends for tapas or drinks (**ir de tapas / de copas**) or to go out in the evening (**ir/salir de marcha**). But you may also be invited over for a meal or a party.

I'm going to organize…	Voy a hacer…	boy ah ah**thayr**
a lunch.	una comida.	oonah ko**mee**dah
a dinner.	una cena.	oonah **thay**nah
a birthday party.	una fiesta de cumpleaños.	oonah **fyes**tah day koomplay**ah**nyos

Do you want to come?	¿Te apetece venir?	tay ahpay**tay**thay bay**neer**
Of course, I'll be very happy to come.	Por supuesto, iré con mucho gusto.	por soo**pwes**to ee**ray** kon **moo**cho **goo**sto
I'm sorry, I have another commitment.	Lo siento, tengo un compromiso.	lo **syen**to **ten**go oon kompro**mee**so
Thank you for inviting me.	Gracias por la invitación.	**grah**thyahs por lah eenbeetah**thyon**

We had a great time.
Lo hemos pasado muy bien.
lo **ay**mos pah**sah**do **moo**ee byen

Meeting up …

La cita is a rather formal term for a *date, appointment* or *meeting.* With friends, it's more common to use the verb **quedar** *to arrange to meet* (for work-related terms, see 'Business meetings').

When shall we meet up?
¿Cuándo quedamos?
kwando kay**dah**mos

At what time shall we meet?
¿A qué hora quedamos?
ah kay **o**rah kay**dah**mos

I've arranged to meet some friends.
He quedado con unos amigos.
ay kaydahdo kon oonos ahmeegos

I've made an arrangement for tonight.
He quedado esta noche.
ay kaydahdo estah nochay

I can't, I've already arranged to meet someone.
No puedo, ya he quedado.
no pwaydo yah ay kaydahdo

Have you (informal) *arranged to meet someone?*
¿Has quedado con alguien?
ahs kaydahdo kon ahlgyen

Shall we meet to ...	¿Quedamos para...	kaydahmos pahrah
get a pre-meal drink?	tomar el aperitivo?	tomahr el ahpayreeteebo
go to the cinema?	ir al cine?	eer ahl theenay
go shopping?	ir de compras?	eer day komprahs
have a drink?	tomar una copa?	tomahr oonah kopah
go out clubbing?	ir de marcha?	eer day mahrchah
go out drinking?	ir de copas?	eer day kopahs

... and chatting up

Even though gestures are sometimes enough, a bit of vocabulary can't hurt your chances of impressing. There's a wide choice: traditional, romantic, direct or even poetic. It's up to you to choose your style! In Spain, despite changing times, it's not uncommon to hear young men addressing a compliment (**el piropo**) to a young woman passing by.

Before attempting any seduction, be sure to check out the pros and cons of the situation first!

He/She is hot.	Está bueno/-a / buenísimo/-a.	estah bwayno/-ah / bwayneeseemo/-ah
He/She is a stunner.	Está como un tren. Está como un queso.	estah komo oon tren estah komo oon kayso
He/She is fit.	Está macizo/-a.	estah mahtheetho/-ah
He/She is cute.	Es mono/-a.	es mono/-ah
He/She is a sweetheart.	Es un encanto.	es oon enkahnto
He/She is charming.	Tiene ángel.	tyenay ahnhayl
He/She is very sweet.	Es muy dulce.	es mooee doolthay
He/She is affectionate.	Es tierno/-a.	es tyayrno/-ah
He/She is funny.	Es salado/-a.	es sahlahdo/-ah
He's handsome. / She's beautiful.	Es guapo/-a.	es gwahpo/-ah
He/She is ugly.	Es feo/-a.	es fayo/-ah
He/She is really ugly.	Es un callo. Es un feto. Es un horror de tío/-a.	es oon kahyo es oon fayto es oon orror day teeo/-ah

to pick up	ligar	leegahr
I picked up a hot guy/girl.	He ligado con un tío bueno/una tía buena.	ay leegahdo kon oon teeo bwayno / oonah teeah bwaynah
He's a ladies' man.	Es un ligón (de playa).	es oon leegon day plahyah
He/She is clingy.	Es pegajoso/-a.	es paygahhoso/-ah
He/She is horrible.	Es un cardo.	es oon kahrdo
He can't keep his hands off.	Es un pulpo.	es oon poolpo
He/She fancies me.	Le hago tilín.	lay ahgo teeleen
You fancy him/her.	Te hace tilín.	tay ahthay teeleen
He/She is flirting with me.	Me está tirando los tejos.	may estah teerahndo los tayhos

Do you want to make a declaration of love? You can simply stick with **Te quiero** *I love you*, or take your pick from the below.

I love you–I can't stop thinking about you.
Te quiero, no dejo de pensar en ti.
*tay **kyay**ro no **day**ho day pen**sahr** en tee*

I adore you–I'm losing sleep over you.
Te adoro, me quitas el sueño.
*tay ah**do**ro may **kee**tahs el **sway**nyo*

I'm (m./f.) in love with you.
Estoy enamorado/-a de ti.
*es**toy** enahmo**rah**do/-ah day tee*

I like you–you're lovely.
Me gustas, eres un encanto.
*may **goo**stahs **ay**rays oon en**kahn**to*

Do you fancy going out with me?
¿Te apetece salir conmigo?
*tay ahpay**tay**thay sah**leer** kon**mee**go*

I miss you.
Te echo de menos.
*tay **ay**cho day **may**nos*

I'm (m./f.) crazy about you. / You're everything to me. / I've got you under my skin.
Estoy colado/-a por ti. / Estoy por ti. / Estoy por tus huesos.
*es**toy** ko**lah**do/-ah por tee / es**toy** por tee / es**toy** por toos **way**sos*

If things get to this stage …

	Me he acostado con...	*may ay ahko**stah**do kon*
I slept with ...	Me he liado con...	*may ay **lyah**do kon*
	Me he enrollado con...	*may ay enro**yah**do kon*
	He tenido un rollo con...	*ay ten**ee**do oon **rro**yo kon*

to kiss	besarse	bay**sahr**say
to make out / snog	morrearse	morray**ahr**say
to roll in the hay	darse un revolcón	**dahr**say oon rraybol**kon**
to have a screw / shag	echar un polvo / quiqui	ay**chahr** oon **pol**bo / **kee**kee

… or if they don't, or if you prefer they don't …

I'm not single.	Tengo pareja.	**ten**go pah**ray**hah
He/She turned me down.	Me ha dado calabazas.	may ah **dah**do kahlah**bah**thahs
Are you kidding?	¿De qué vas?	day kay bahs
You're badly mistaken.	Te estás columpiando.	tay es**tahs** koloom**pyahn**do
Leave me alone!	¡Déjame en paz!	**day**hahmay en pahth

And finally, some terms of endearment:

'darling' / 'my darling'	cariño / cariño mío	kah**reen**yo / **mee**o
'my love'	mi amor	mee ah**mor**
'my life'	mi vida	mee **bee**dah
'beautiful'	cara bonita	**kah**rah bo**nee**tah
'gorgeous'	precioso/-a	pray**thyo**so/-ah

↗ Time and the calendar

Telling the time

In Spanish, you don't ask the 'time', you ask the 'hour' (**la hora**).

What time is it?
¿Qué hora es?
kay orah es

Do you (formal) know what time it is, please?
¿Tiene usted hora, por favor?
tyenay ooste^d orah por fahbor

What time do you close?
¿A qué hora cerráis?
ah kay orah thayrrahees

What time does the train leave?
¿A qué hora sale el tren?
ah kay orah sahlay el tren

The 24-hour clock is not often used in speech. The hours are given from 1 to 12, sometimes specifying **de la mañana**, **de la tarde** or **de la noche**. Also, be aware that in Spain if someone arranges to meet you at **mediodía** *noon*, *midday*, this could well mean 1:00 or even 2:00 p.m.!

It's 12:25 at night.
Son las doce y veinticinco (de la noche).
son lahs dothay ee byenteetheenko day lah nochay

It's exactly 1:00 a.m.
Es la una en punto (de la mañana).
es lah oonah en poonto day lah mahnyahnah

It's a quarter to three (in the morning).
Son las tres menos cuarto (de la mañana).
son lahs tres maynos kwahrto day lah mahnyahnah

It's five past twelve (in the morning).
Son las doce y cinco (de la mañana).
son lahs dothay ee theenko day lah mahnyahnah

It's a quarter past one (in the afternoon).
Es la una y cuarto (de la tarde).
es lah oonah ee kwahrto day lah tahrday

It's twenty to five (in the afternoon).
Son las cinco menos veinte (de la tarde).
*son lahs **theen**ko **may**nos **bay**eentay day lah **tahr**day*

It's half past six (in the evening).
Son las seis y media (de la tarde).
*son lahs **say**ees ee **may**dyah day lah **tahr**day*

It's ten past ten (at night).
Son las diez y diez (de la noche).
*son lahs dyeth ee dyeth day lah **no**chay*

Days, months, time and the seasons

Days of the week and months are not capitalized in Spanish. Also,
de *of* is put in front of the month and the year: *28 March 2015* is
28 de marzo de 2015.

What day is it today?
¿Qué día es hoy?
*kay **dee**ah es oy*

It's Monday, the 28th of March.
Es lunes, 28 de marzo.
*es **loo**nays **bay**eentay **o**cho day **mahr**tho*

Days of the week

Monday	lunes	**loo**nays
Tuesday	martes	**mahr**tays
Wednesday	miércoles	**myayr**kolays
Thursday	jueves	**hway**bays
Friday	viernes	**byayr**nays
Saturday	sábado	**sah**bahdo
Sunday	domingo	do**meen**go

Months of the year

January	**enero**	*en**ay**ro*
February	**febrero**	*feb**ray**ro*
March	**marzo**	***mahr**tho*
April	**abril**	*ah**breel***
May	**mayo**	***mah**yo*
June	**junio**	***hoo**nyo*
July	**julio**	***hoo**lyo*
August	**agosto**	*ah**gos**to*
September	**septiembre**	*sep**tyem**bray*
October	**octubre**	*ok**too**bray*
November	**noviembre**	*no**byem**bray*
December	**diciembre**	*dee**thyem**bray*

Talking about 'when' and 'how often'

after(wards)	**después (de)**	*des**pways** day*
already	**ya**	*yah*
always	**siempre**	***syem**pray*
before	**antes (de)**	***ahn**tays day*
during	**durante**	*doo**rahn**tay*
early	**temprano**	*tem**prahn**o*
every day	**cada día**	***kah**dah **dee**ah*
first	**primero**	*pree**may**ro*
from time to time	**de vez en cuando**	*day beth en **kwahn**do*
immediately / right now	**ya / enseguida / ahora mismo**	*yah / ensay**ghee**dah / ahorah **mees**mo*
in the end / finally	**al final / finalmente**	*ahl fee**nahl** / feenahl**men**tay*
in three days	**dentro de tres días**	***den**tro day tres **dee**ahs*
late	**tarde**	***tahr**day*
later	**luego / más tarde**	***lway**go / mahs **tahr**day*
meanwhile	**mientras tanto**	***myen**trahs **tahn**to*

never	nunca / jamás	noonkah / hahmahs
now	ahora	ahorah
often	a menudo	ah menoodo
once a year	una vez al año	oonah beth ahl ahnyo
quickly	rápido / deprisa	rrahpeedo / daypreesah
rarely	pocas veces	pokahs baythays
slowly	despacio	despahthyo
sometimes	a veces	ah baythays
then	entonces	entonthays
twice a day	dos veces al día	dos baythays ahl deeah
two days ago	hace dos días	ahthay dos deeahs

More time words ...

birthday	cumpleaños (m.)	koomplayahnyos
dawn / daybreak	amanecer (m.)	ahmahnaythayr
day	día (m.)	deeah
dusk	atardecer (m.)	ahtahrdaythayr
last night	anoche	ahnochay
month	mes (m.)	mays
next year	el año que viene	el ahnyo kay byenay
nightfall	anochecer (m.)	ahnochaythayr
Saint's day	el santo (m.)	el sahnto
the day after tomorrow	pasado mañana	pahsahdo mahnyahnah
the day before yesterday	anteayer	ahntayahyayr
the night before last	anteanoche	ahntayahnochay
today	hoy	oy
tomorrow	mañana	mahnyahnah
week	semana (f.)	saymahnah
weekend	fin (m.) de semana	feen day saymahnah
weekly	semanal	saymahnahl

year	**año** *(m.)*	*ahnyo*
yesterday	**ayer**	*ahyayr*
to stay up late	**trasnochar**	*trahsnochahr*
to get up early	**madrugar**	*mahdroogahr*

Note that in Spanish, to say *in the morning/evening/night*, **por** is used rather than 'in'. **Por la mañana, me tomo un café con leche.** *In the morning, I have a coffee with milk.*

at dawn	**de madrugada**	*day mahdroogahdah*
in the morning	**por la mañana**	*por lah mahnyahnah*
at midday / noon	**a mediodía**	*ah medyodeeah*
in the afternoon / evening	**por la tarde**	*por lah tahrday*
at night	**por la noche**	*por lah nochay*

The seasons

season	**estación** *(f.)*	*estahthyon*
spring	**primavera** *(f.)*	*preemahbayrah*
summer	**verano** *(m.)*	*bayrahno*
autumn	**otoño** *(m.)*	*otonyo*
winter	**invierno** *(m.)*	*eenbyayrno*

Festivals and holidays

Spain has ten national holidays, with three falling in December, making it a particularly festive month. On 6 January, the holiday of **Día de Reyes** (Epiphany), celebrating the coming of the Three Kings (or Magi) to the baby Jesus, is almost as important as Christmas. On the eve of this day there are parades, and in the morning children receive presents.

1 January: **Año Nuevo** *New Year's Day*
6 January: **Día de Reyes** *Three Kings Day*
March–April: **Viernes Santo** *Good Friday*
1 May: **Fiesta del Trabajo** *Labour Day*
15 August: **La Virgen** *The Assumption*
12 October: **Día de la Hispanidad** *Hispanic Heritage Day* (Spain's national holiday commemorating the arrival of Christopher Columbus in the Americas)
1 November: **Todos los Santos** *All Saints' Day*
6 December: **Día de la Constitución** *Constitution Day (1978)*
8 December: **Fiesta de la Inmaculada** *Immaculate Conception*
25 December: **Navidad** *Christmas*

During the year, there are four other public holidays: two for each **Comunidad Autónoma**, and two for each locality. Each town or village celebrates the day of its patron saint, e.g. **San Isidro** in Madrid (15 May); **la Mercè** in Barcelona (24 September), etc.

↗ **Asking for assistance**

Emergencies

In case of emergency, the **teléfono de emergencias** *emergency number* is 112: it is free and forwards all calls to the appropriate service. Here are a few helpful phrases if you need assistance:

Help!	**¡Socorro!**	*so**ko**rro*
	¡Auxilio!	*aoo**see**lyo*
	¡Ayuda!	*ah**yoo**dah*
Fire!	**¡Fuego!**	***fway**go*

Quick, call ...	**¡Rápido, llamen...**	***rrah**peedo **yah**men*
an ambulance!	**una ambulancia!**	*oo**nah** ahmboo**lahn**thyah*
a doctor!	**a un médico!**	*ah oon **may**deeko*

the police!	**a la policía!**	*ah lah poleetheeah*
the fire service!	**a los bomberos!**	*ah los bombayros*

Someone is injured.	**Hay un herido.**	*I oon ayreedo*
There's a lot of smoke.	**Hay mucho humo.**	*I moocho oomo*
There's flooding.	**Hay una inundación.**	*I oonah eenoondahthyon*

On the road

If you have a breakdown or accident:

I need a tow truck to be sent to kilometre ... of the motorway because ...	**Necesito que me envíen una grúa al km.... de la autopista porque...**	*naythayseeto kay may enbeeen oonah grooah ahl keelomaytro ... day lah aootopeestah porkay*
my car has broken down.	**tengo una avería.**	*tengo oonah ahbayreeah*
I've had an accident.	**he tenido un accidente.**	*ay teneedo oon ahktheedentay*
I can't start my car.	**no puedo arrancar el coche.**	*no pwaydo ahrrahnkahr el kochay*
I've run out of petrol / gasoline.	**me he quedado sin gasolina.**	*may ay kaydahdo seen gahsoleenah*
I have two flat tires.	**he pinchado dos ruedas.**	*ay peenchahdo dos rrwaydahs*
I don't have a spare tire.	**no llevo rueda de recambio.**	*no yaybo rrwaydah day rraykahmbyo*

Signs, notices and abbreviations

Signs and notices

Arrivals	**Llegadas**	*yaygahdahs*
Beware of the dog	**Cuidado con el perro**	*kweedahdo kon el payrro*
Closed	**Cerrado**	*thayrrahdo*

Danger	**Peligro**	*pay**lee**gro*
Departures	**Salidas**	*sah**lee**dahs*
Emergency exit	**Salida de emergencia**	*sah**lee**dah day emayr**hen**thyah*
Floor	**Planta**	***plahn**tah*
Ladies' room (toilets)	**Damas**	***dah**mahs*
Local trains	**Cercanías**	*thayrkah**nee**ahs*
Men's room (toilets)	**Caballeros**	*kahbah**yay**ros*
No cell/mobile phones	**Prohibido el uso de móvil**	*proee**bee**do el **oo**so day **mo**beel*
No littering	**Prohibido tirar basura**	*proee**bee**do tee**rahr** bah**soo**rah*
No parking	**No aparcar**	*no ahpahr**kahr***
Open	**Abierto**	*ah**byayr**to*
Post office	**Correos**	*ko**rray**os*
Pull	**Tiren**	***tee**ren*
Push	**Empujen**	*em**poo**hen*
Sale	**Rebajas**	*rray**bah**hahs*
Station	**Estación**	*estah**thyon***
Ticket office	**Taquilla**	*tah**kee**yah*
Toilets / restrooms	**Servicios**	*sayr**bee**thyos*

In the autonomous communities with an official regional language, roadsigns are generally bilingual. In the Basque Country, the names of towns are given in Spanish and Basque: **San Sebastián / Donostia**; **Vitoria / Gasteiz**; **Pamplona / Iruña**. Some signs appear in the local language only. For example, **calle** *street* is *carrer* in Catalonia (and in some places in Valencia and Mallorca), *rúa* in Galicia and *kalea* in the Basque Country.

Abbreviations

Here are a few abbreviations you might see, especially on letters.

D.	**Don** *Sir* (courtesy title)
D.ª	**Doña** *Madam* (courtesy title)
Sr.	**Señor** *Mr*
Sra.	**Señora** *Mrs*
Srta.	**Señorita** *Miss*
Avda.	**Avenida** *Avenue*
Pza.	**Plaza** *Square*
C/	**Calle** *Street*
S/N	**Sin número** *No number*
Ud or **Vd**	**Usted** *you* (formal sing.)

When the initials refer to plural words, the letter is doubled: **SS.MM = Sus Majestades** *Their Royal Majesties* (Spain has a king and queen); **EE.UU = Estados Unidos** *United States*, etc.

AVE [*ah*bay]	**Alta Velocidad Española** *Spanish high-speed train*
DNI [*daye*nay**ee**]	**Documento Nacional de Identidad** *National identity card*. In administrative contexts, someone might be asked: **¿Me permite su DNI, por favor?** *May I see your identity card please?*
IVA [*ee*bah]	**Impuesto sobre el Valor Añadido** *sales tax, value-added tax*
ONCE [*on*thay]	**Organización Nacional de Ciegos Españoles** On streets across Spain, you will see small ONCE (*National Organization for the Blind*) stands, where lottery tickets (**los cupones**) are sold.

| **PP** | **Partido Popular** *Popular* or *People's Party* |
| [pay**pay**] | (conservative political party) |

| **PSOE** | **Partido Socialista Obrero Español** *Spanish* |
| [pay**so**ay] | *Socialist Workers' Party* (social democratic party) |

| **RENFE** | **Red Nacional de Ferrocarriles de España** |
| [**rren**fay] | *National Network of Spanish Railways* |

↗ Travelling

Passport control and customs

Citizens of the European Union can enter Spain with a valid ID card or a passport. A passport is required for non-EU citizens, but a visa is only necessary for certain countries or if a visitor is staying for more than 90 days.

Your passport, please.
Su pasaporte, por favor.
soo pahsah**por**tay por fah**bor**

Do you have anything to declare?
¿Tiene usted algo que declarar?
tyenay oo**ste**ᵈ **ahl**go kay dayklah**rahr**

Can you open your suitcase, please?
¿Puede abrir la maleta, por favor?
pwayday ah**breer** lah mah**lay**tah por fah**bor**

How long are you going to stay?
¿Qué tiempo va a durar su estancia?
kay **tyem**po bah ah doo**rahr** soo es**tahn**thyah

I'm going to ...	Voy a...	voy ah
stay for 15 days.	estar quince días.	estahr keenthay deeahs
live here for a year.	residir durante un año.	rrayseedeer doorahntay oon ahnyo

I'm coming ...	Vengo...	bengo
to study.	por un tema de estudios.	por oon taymah day estoodyos
as a tourist.	de turismo.	day tooreesmo
for business.	por motivos de trabajo.	por moteebos day trahbahho

Money

Can you change these traveller's cheques / British pounds / American dollars for me?
¿Puede cambiarme estos cheques de viaje / estas libras esterlinas / estos dólares americanos?
pwayday kahmbyahrmay estos chaykays day byahhay / estahs leebrahs estayrleenahs / estos dolahrays ahmayreekahnos

What is ...	¿Cuál es...	kwahl es
the commission?	la comisión?	lah komeesyon
the exchange rate?	el tipo de cambio?	el teepo day kambyo

Flying

Airports are multilingual environments, but here are some useful phrases for communicating with airline staff if need be.

Do you prefer a window or an aisle seat?
¿Prefiere ventanilla o pasillo?
prayfyayray bentahneeyah o pahseeyo

Do you have baggage to check in?
¿Tiene usted algún equipaje para facturar?
tyenay ooste^d ahlgoon aykeepahhay pahrah fahktoorahr

Can I carry this luggage with me?
¿Puedo llevar este equipaje conmigo?
pwaydo yaybahr estay aykeepahhay konmeego

Is the flight late?
¿Tiene retraso el vuelo?
tyenay rraytrahso el bwaylo

From which terminal does flight ... leave?
¿De qué terminal sale el vuelo...?
day kay tayrmeenahl sahlay el bwaylo

I've missed the plane.
He perdido el avión.
ay payrdeedo el ahbyon

backrest	respaldo (m.) del asiento	rrespaldo del ahsyento
baggage	equipaje (m.)	aykeepahhay
boarding gate	puerta (f.) de embarque	pwayrto day embahrkay
boarding pass	tarjeta (f.) de embarque	tahrhaytah day embahrkay
cart / trolley	carrito (m.)	kahrreeto
to check in	facturar	fahktoorahr
counter	mostrador (m.)	mostrahdor
crew	tripulación (f.)	treepoolahthyon
destination	destino (m.)	desteeno
flight	vuelo (m.)	bwaylo

onboard personnel	**personal** (m.) **de a bordo**	*payrsonahl day ah **bor**do*
safety belt	**cinturón** (m.) **de seguridad**	*theentooron day saygooreedah^d*
seat	**asiento** (m.)	*ahsyento*
stopover	**escala** (f.)	*eskahlah*
to take off	**despegar**	*despay**gahr***
terminal	**terminal** (f.)	*tayrmee**nahl***
ticket	**billete** (m.)	*beeyaytay*
... single	**... de ida**	*day eedah*
... return	**... de ida y vuelta**	*day eedah ee **bwayl**tah*
visa	**visado** (m.)	*bee**sah**do*

Going by bus or train

RENFE, the railway company, has high-speed trains (**AVE**) between Madrid and several large cities. Regular-speed trains will get you to most other destinations comfortably and quickly. There is also an extensive network of long-distance coaches – travelling by bus is often significantly cheaper.

Where is the railway/bus station?
¿Dónde está la estación de tren / autobuses?
*don*day es*tah* lah estah*thyon* day tren / aooto*boo*says

What time does the first / next / last bus (train) leave for ...?
¿A qué hora sale el primer / el próximo / el último autocar (tren) para...?
ah kay orah sahlay el preemayr / el prokseemo / el oolteemo aootokahr tren pahrah

I'd like a ticket to ...
Quisiera un billete para...
keesyayrah oon beeyaytay pahrah

How long is the journey?
¿Cuánto tiempo dura el trayecto?
kwahnto tyempo doorah el trahyekto

To go to ... you must change in ...
Para ir a..., tiene que hacer transbordo en...
pahrah eer ah tyenay kay ahthayr trahnsbordo en

How are you going to pay?
¿Cómo va a pagar?
komo bah ah pahgahr

In cash.
En metálico. / En efectivo.
en maytahleeko en efekteebo

With a card.
Con tarjeta.
kon tahrhaytah

bay / platform (bus)	**dársena** *(f.)*	*dahrsaynah*
car	**coche** *(m.)*	*kochay*
counter	**mostrador** *(m.)*	*mostrahdor*
discount	**descuento** *(m.)*	*deskwento*
first class	**preferente**	*prayfayrentay*
local train	**cercanías** *(m.)*	*thayrkahneeahs*
long distance	**largo recorrido**	*lahrgo rraykorreedo*
platform (train)	**andén** *(m.)*	*ahnden*
seat	**asiento** *(m.)*	*ahsyento*
second class	**turista**	*tooreestah*
sleeper berth	**litera** *(f.)*	*leetayrah*
sleeping car	**coche cama** *(m.)*	*kochay kahmah*
ticket window	**ventanilla** *(f.)*	*bentahneeyah*

Going by boat

From Britain, you can travel to Spain by ferry. Once in Spain, there are ferries to numerous destinations: Italy, North Africa and, of course, the Balearic and Canary Islands.

accommodation	acomodación (f.)	ahkomodah**thyon**
cabin with bathroom	cabina (f.) con baño	kah**bee**nah kon **bah**nyo
cabin with two / four beds	camarote (m.) de dos / cuatro camas	kahmah**ro**tay day dos / **kwah**tro **kah**mahs
camper / motor home	autocaravana (f.)	aootokahrah**bah**nah
deck	cubierta (f.)	koo**byayr**tah
dock	dársena (f.)	**dahr**saynah
hold	bodega (f.)	bo**day**gah
reclining seat	butaca (f.)	boo**tah**kah

Going by taxi

If you give an exact address, in Spain the name of the street comes first, followed by the number: **Voy a Serrano 54**. As for tipping the driver, you are not expected to give **una propina** *a tip* of a specific percentage; you can simply round up the amount.

Hello, I'd like a taxi for 34 Embajadores Street, reserved in the name of Andrés Hernández. I'm in a bit of a hurry.
Buenas tardes, quisiera un taxi a Embajadores 34, a nombre de Andrés Hernández. Tengo algo de prisa.
*bway*nahs **tahr**days kee**syay**rah oon **tah**ksee ah embahhah**do**rays
*tray*eentah ee **kwah**tro ah **nom**bray day … **ten**go **ahl**go day **pree**sah

How much do I owe you (formal)?
¿Qué le debo?
*kay lay **day**bo*

Do you (formal) *have change?*		*I don't have any change.*
¿Tiene cambio?		**No llevo suelto.**
*tyen*ay **kahm**byo		*no* **yay**bo **swel**to

Biking and motorcycling

Montar en bicicleta *biking* or **motocicleta** *motorcycling* is one way to discover Spain in the open air. You might also hear the shortened forms **la bici** *[beethee] bike* and **la moto** *motorbike*. Larger towns often have **carriles bici** *bicycle lanes* – pedestrians should avoid them if they don't want a fine!

anti-theft device	**antirrobo** *(m.)*	*ahnteerrobo*
brake	**freno** *(m.)*	***fray*no**
chain	**cadena** *(f.)*	*kah**day**nah*
handlebars	**manillar** *(m.)*	*mahnee**yahr***
light	**faro** *(m.)*	***fah*ro**
lightbulb	**bombilla** *(f.)*	*bom**bee**yah*
pedal	**pedal** *(m.)*	*pay**dahl***
seat (cycle)	**sillín** *(m.)*	*see**yeen***
speed / gear	**marcha** *(f.)*	***mahr*chah**

Renting a car

I'd like to rent a car for a day / a weekend / a week.

Quisiera alquilar un coche para un día / un fin de semana / una semana.

*kee**syay**rah ahlkee**lahr** oon **ko**chay **pah**rah oon **dee**ah / oon feen day say**mah**nah / **oo**nah say**mah**nah*

What models do you have?

¿Qué modelos tiene?

*kay mo**day**los **tyen**ay*

Does the price include unlimited mileage?
¿La tarifa incluye kilometraje ilimitado?
*lah tah**ree**fah een**kloo**yay keelomay**trah**hay eeleemee**tah**do*

Is it possible to rent a car here and return it in Malaga?
¿Es posible alquilar un coche aquí y devolverlo en Málaga?
*es po**see**blay ahlkee**lahr** oon **ko**chay ah**kee** ee daybol**bayr**lo en …*

Driving

Spain's motorways/freeways (**autopistas**) have tolls (**peajes**), which in some regions (notably Catalonia) are quite expensive. Highways/dual carriageways (**autovías**) are free. Distances and speeds are given in kilometres: the maximum speed on most motorways is 120 km/h (about 75 mph).

antifreeze	**anticongelante** (m.)	*anteekonhay**lahn**tay*
brake fluid	**líquido** (m.) **de frenos**	*lee**kee**do day **fray**nos*
diesel	**gasoil** (m.)	*gah**so**eel*
full (tank)	**lleno**	***yay**no*
oil can	**lata** (f.) **de aceite**	***lah**tah de ah**thay**eetay*
petrol / gasoline	**gasolina** (f.)	*gahso**lee**nah*
petrol/gas station	**gasolinera** (f.)	*gahsolee**nay**rah*
petrol/gas tank	**depósito** (m.)	*day**po**seeto*

Most petrol stations are self-service; first you pay the cashier, then you fill up your tank. (There are almost 4 litres in a gallon.)

A full tank, please.
Lleno, por favor.
yay**no por fah**bor

I'm going to put in 20 litres.
Voy a poner veinte litros.
*voy ah po**nayr** bay**een**tay **lee**tros*

Could you check ...	¿Podría revisar...	podreeah rraybeesahr
the battery?	la batería?	lah bahtayreeah
the brakes?	los frenos?	los fraynos
the brake pads?	las pastillas de freno?	lahs pasteeyahs day frayno
the clutch?	el embrague?	el embrahgay
the gear box?	la caja de cambios?	lah kahhah day kambyos
the lights?	las luces?	lahs loothays
the oil level?	el nivel de aceite?	el neebel day ahthayeetay
the tire pressure?	la presión de las ruedas?	lah praysyon day lahs rrwaydahs

Hopefully you won't have any problems, but if you do:

accident	accidente (m.)	ahktheedentay
accident report	parte (m.) de accidente	pahrtay day ahktheedentay
all-risk coverage	a todo riesgo	ah todo rryesgo
driving licence	carné (m.) de conducir	kahrnay day kondootheer
to fill in a report	rellenar un parte	rrayyaynahr oon pahrtay
fine	multa (f.)	mooltah
insurance	seguro (m.)	saygooro
joint accident report	parte (m.) amistoso	pahrtay ahmeestoso
to lose licence points	quitar puntos	keetahr poontos
no overtaking / no passing	adelantamiento (m.) prohibido	ahdaylahntahmyento proeebeedo
road signs	señales (f.)	saynyahlays
seatbelt	cinturón (m.) de seguridad	theentooron day saygooreedaᵈ
speeding	exceso (m.) de velocidad	eksthayso day baylotheedaᵈ
third-party coverage	a terceros	ah tayrthayros
tow truck	grúa (f.)	grooah
wheel clamp	cepo (m.)	thaypo

↗ Getting around town

Finding your way around

How can I get to the town centre, please?
Por favor, ¿cómo puedo ir al centro?
por fahbor komo pwaydo eer ahl thentro

Is there a pharmacy near here?
¿Hay alguna farmacia cerca de aquí?
I ahlgoonah fahrmahthyah thayrkah day ahkee

Excuse me, where is the Prado museum?
Perdone, ¿dónde queda el museo del Prado?
payrdonay donday kaydah el moosayo del prahdo

Giving someone directions

Continue straight ahead.
Siga todo recto.
seegah todo rrekto

Go to the roundabout.
Vaya hasta la rotonda.
bahyah ahstah lah rrotondah

Take the second exit on the right.
Tome la segunda salida a la derecha.
tomay lah saygoondah sahleedah ah lah dayraychah

It's the first street on the left.
Es la primera calle a la izquierda.
es lah preemayrah kahyay ah lah eethkyayrdah

Taking public transport

Madrid and Barcelona have an extensive underground/subway system for getting around the city.

change / transfer	**transbordo** (m.)	*trahnsbordo*
to change	**transbordar**	*trahnsbordahr*
connection	**correspondencia** (f.)	*korrespondenthyah*
direction	**destino** (m.)	*desteeno*
platform	**andén** (m.)	*ahnden*
stop (bus, tram, metro)	**parada** (f.)	*pahrahdah*
ticket	**billete** (m.)	*beeyaytay*
ticket window	**ventanilla** (f.)	*bentahneeyah*

The nearest metro station, please?
¿La estación de metro más cercana, por favor?
lah estahthyon day maytro mahs thayrkahnah por fahbor

Where is the stop for the 61 bus?
¿Dónde está la parada del 61?
donday estah lah pahrahdah del saysentah ee oono

What line should I take for … ?
¿Qué línea tengo que coger para…?
kay leenayah tengo kay kohayr pahrah

What bus should I take for … ?
¿Qué autobús tengo que coger para…?
kay aootoboos tengo kay kohayr pahrah

Where should I get off for … ?
¿Dónde tengo que bajar para…?
donday tengo kay bahhahr pahrah

Going to the museum

Spain is teeming with museums and historical sites of interest.
Just to give one example, Madrid has the greatest concentration

of artworks in Europe in the **triángulo del arte** *art triangle* formed by its three world-famous fine art museums: El Prado, the Thyssen-Bornemisza and the Reina Sofía.

I'd like two tickets.
Quisiera dos entradas.
kee**syay**rah dos en**trah**dahs

Is there any kind of discount for ...	¿Hay algún tipo de descuento para...	I ahl**goon tee**po day des**kwen**to **pah**rah
students?	estudiantes?	estoo**dyahn**tays
teachers?	profesores?	profay**so**rays
children under twelve?	niños menores de doce años?	**neen**yos may**nor**ays day **do**thay **ah**nyos
senior citizens?	jubilados?	hoobee**lah**dos

Can we take photos?
¿Se pueden hacer fotos?
say **pway**den ah**thayr fo**tos

Places of interest

Spain ranks third in the world in number of UNESCO World Heritage sites. Locations that have received this designation include landscapes, monuments and even entire city districts; for example, the Moorish **Albaicín** quarter (**el barrio**) in Granada, the historic city of Toledo, and Córdoba's old town.

castle	**castillo** *(m.)*	kah**stee**yo
cathedral	**catedral** *(f.)*	kahtay**drahl**
church	**iglesia** *(f.)*	ee**glay**syah
flea market (in Madrid)	**el Rastro**	el **rrah**stro
historic centre	**casco** *(m.)* **histórico**	**kah**sko ee**sto**reeko

Jewish quarter (historic)	judería (f.)	hooday**ree**ah
mosque	mezquita (f.)	meth**kee**tah
palace	palacio (m.)	pah**lah**thyo
synagogue	sinagoga (f.)	seenah**go**gah
traditional neighbourhood	barrio (m.) típico	**bah**rryo tee**pee**ko
wall	muralla (f.)	moo**rah**yah
zoo	zoológico (m.)	tho-o**lo**heeko

Posting a letter

To send a letter (**una carta**) or a postcard (**una postal**), you can buy a stamp (**un sello**) at a tobacconist's (**un estanco**) and take it to the post office (**Correos**) or put it in a postbox (**un buzón**).

Excuse me, do you know where there is ...	Por favor, ¿sabe dónde hay...	por fah**bor** sah**bay** **don**day I
a post office?	una oficina de Correos?	**oo**nah ofee**thee**nah day ko**rray**os
a tobacconist's near here?	un estanco por aquí?	oon es**tahn**ko por ah**kee**
a postbox in this area?	un buzón en esta zona?	oon boo**thon** en **estah** **tho**nah

I need an envelope and a stamp for Australia / the United Kingdom / the United States / Canada / Ireland / New Zealand / South Africa.

Necesito un sobre y un sello para Australia / el Reino Unido / Estados Unidos / Canadá / Irlanda / Nueva Zelanda / Sudáfrica.

*naythay**see**to oon **sob**ray ee oon **sayy**o **pah**rah aoo**strah**lyah / el rray**ee**no oo**nee**do / e**stah**dos oo**nee**dos / kahnah**dah** / eer**lahn**dah / **nway**bah thay**lahn**dah / sood**ah**freeka*

98

I'd like to send this parcel by standard post / express post / registered post.

Quisiera mandar este paquete por correo normal / urgente / certificado.

*kee**syay**rah mahn**dahr** es**tay** pah**kay**tay por ko**rray**o nor**mahl** / oor**hen**tay / thayrteefee**kah**do*

Making a phone call

Although pay phones are rarer with the advent of mobile phones, you can still find telephone boxes/booths (**cabinas**) on the street. Spain also has many call shops (**locutorios**), which have private booths to make calls and then you pay afterwards at the counter. Pre-paid cards (**tarjetas prepago**) are the cheapest option.

code	**código** (m.)	**ko**deego
to dial	**marcar**	mahr**kahr**
dialling code	**prefijo** (m.)	pray**fee**ho
digit	**dígito** (m.)	**dee**heeto
extension	**extensión** (f.)	eksten**syon**
hash key / pound sign	**almohadilla** (f.)	ahlmoah**dee**yah
information	**información** (f.)	eenformah**thyon**
key	**tecla** (f.)	**tay**klah
keypad (telephone)	**teclado** (m.)	tay**klah**do
mobile / cell phone	**móvil** (m.)	**mo**beel
network coverage	**cobertura** (f.)	kobayr**too**rah
to press	**pulsar**	pool**sahr**
star key	**asterisco** (m.)	ahstay**rees**ko

(The person answering)
Yes, hello?
Sí, dígame. (formal)
*see **dee**gahmay*

Sí, dime. (informal)
*see **dee**may*

Good afternoon/evening, is Antonio there?

Buenas tardes, ¿está Antonio?

bwaynahs tahrdays estah antonyo

Who is speaking?

¿De parte de quién?

day pahrtay day kyen

This is Mario.

De parte de Mario.

day pahrtay day mahryo

The number you have dialled is engaged/busy or out of range.

El teléfono al que llama está ocupado o fuera de cobertura.

el taylayfono ahl kay yahmah estah okoopahdo o fwayrah day kobayrtoorah

Leave me a missed call and I'll call you back.

Dame un toque y te vuelvo a llamar.

dahmay oon tokay ee tay bwelbo ah yahmahr

Déjame una llamada perdida y te vuelvo a llamar.

dayhahmay oonah yahmahdah payrdeedah ee tay bwelbo ah yahmahr

Going online

Many establishments have wireless networks (called **wi-fi**, pronounced *[wee-fee]*) if you need to go online.

Is there an internet connection in the hotel?

¿Hay conexión a Internet en el hotel?

I koneksyon ah eentayrnet en el otel

Could you give me the name of the network and the password?

¿Me dice el nombre de la red y la clave?

may deethay el nombray day lah rre^d ee lah klahbay

Do you know if there's an internet café around here?
¿Sabe si hay algún cíber por aquí?
sahbay see I ahlgoon theebayr por ahkee

Which computer should I use?
¿En qué ordenador me pongo?
en kay ordaynahdor may pongo

Can you print this file for me?
¿Me puede imprimir este archivo?
may pwayday eempreemeer estay ahrcheebo

Reporting a theft or loss

In a city, if you have been the victim of a theft or have lost something, go to **la comisaría** *the police station*. In more rural areas, **la Guardia Civil** *Civil Guard* (part of the military) deals with law enforcement.

I want to file a police report.
Quiero poner una denuncia.
kyayro ponayr oonah daynoonthyah

Someone has snatched my bag.
Me han dado un tirón.
may ahn dahdo oon teeron

I've lost ... Someone has stolen ...	He perdido... Me han robado...	ay payrdeedo may ahn rrobahdo
my car.	el coche.	el kochay
my credit card.	la tarjeta de crédito.	lah tahrhaytah day kraydeeto
my documents.	la documentación.	lah dokoomentahthyon
my keys.	las llaves.	lahs yahbays
my mobile/cell phone.	el móvil.	el mobeel

my traveller's cheques.	los cheques de viaje.	los **chay**kays day **byah**hay
my wallet / purse.	la cartera.	lah kahr**tay**rah
the money that I was carrying.	el dinero que llevaba.	el dee**nay**ro kay yay**bah**bah

At the bank

Banks are not open in the afternoon: the standard hours are 9 a.m. to 2 p.m.

Where is there ...	¿Dónde hay...	**don**day I
a bank?	un banco?	oon **bahn**ko
an ATM / cash dispenser?	un cajero automático?	oon kah**hay**ro aooto**mah**teeko

Here are some useful expressions for transactions, which you can precede with **Quisiera**... *I'd like* ...

to change some traveller's cheques	cambiar cheques de viaje	kahm**byahr chay**kays day **byah**hay
to cash a cheque	cobrar un talón	ko**brahr** oon tah**lon**
to make	hacer...	ah**thayr** oon een**gray**so
... a deposit	un ingreso en cuenta	en **kwen**tah
... a cash withdrawal	una disposición en efectivo	**oo**nah deesposee**thyon** en efek**tee**bo
to transfer some money	hacer una transferencia	ah**thayr oo**nah trahnsfay**ren**thyah

Going to a performance

In the context of a performance, a ticket is **una entrada** (in contrast to a ticket for transport, which is **un billete**).

What films are showing?
¿Qué películas están echando?
*kay pay**lee**koolahs es**tahn** ay**chahn**do*

Is there anything interesting on at the theatre?
¿Ponen alguna obra interesante en el teatro?
ponen ahlgoonah obrah eentayraysahntay en el tayahtro

Could I have three tickets for ... ?
¿Me da tres entradas para...?
may dah tres entrahdahs pahrah

At the hairdresser's

If you need your hair coiffed, just **pedir cita** *make an appointment* at **la peluquería** *the hairdresser's.*

Hello, could I make an appointment for today?
Hola, buenos días, ¿me puede dar hora para hoy?
olah bwaynos deeahs may pwayday dahr orah pahrah oy

I would like ...	Quiero...	kyayro
my hair cut.	cortarme el pelo.	kortahrmay el paylo
my hair dyed.	teñirme el pelo.	taynyeermay el paylo

beard	**barba** *(f.)*	**bahr**bah
blond	**rubio**	**rroo**byo
brown	**castaño**	kah**stah**nyo
ends	**puntas** *(f.)*	**poon**tahs
fringe / bangs	**flequillo** *(m.)*	flay**kee**yo
goatee	**perilla** *(f.)*	pay**ree**yah
highlights	**con reflejos**	kon rray**flay**hos
layered	**en capas**	en **kah**pahs
long	**largo**	**lahr**go
not very short	**no muy corto**	no **mooee korto**
shampoo	**champú**	chahm**poo**
to shave	**afeitar**	ahfayee**tahr**

short	**corto**	*korto*
shoulder-length	**por el hombro**	*por el ombro*
sideburns	**patillas** (f.)	*pahteeyahs*
streaks	**mechas** (f.)	*maychahs*
to style	**peinar**	*payeenahr*

⌐ **Outdoor activities**

Recreation

Whether you're planning to surf in Tarifa, ski in Andalusia's Sierra Nevada or in the Pyrenees, or walk the famous **Camino de Santiago** *Way of St. James*, you'll be spoiled for choice in Spain.

How far is the next town?
¿A qué distancia queda el próximo pueblo?
ah kay deestahnthyah kaydah el prokseemo pwayblo

Is there a refuge for hikers near here?
¿Hay algún albergue para senderistas por aquí cerca?
I ahlgoon ahlbayrgay pahrah sendayreestahs por ahkee thayrkah

Is there an area where you can light a fire?
¿Hay alguna zona donde se pueda hacer fuego?
I ahlgoonah thonah donday say pwaydah ahthayr fwaygo

We are pilgrims: are there any beds left in the hostel for the night?
Somos peregrinos: ¿quedan camas en el albergue para pasar la noche?
somos payraygreenos kaydahn kahmahs en el ahlbayrgay pahrah pahsahr lah nochay

We are lost: how do you get to ... ?
Nos hemos perdido: ¿cómo se llega a...?
*nos **ay**mos payr**dee**do **ko**mo say **yay**gah ah*

Could you lend me ...	¿Puedes prestarme...	*pwaydays prestahrmay*
a bottle opener?	**un abrebotellas?**	*oon ahbraybotayyahs*
a box of matches?	**una caja de cerillas?**	*oonah kahhah day thayreeyahs*
a corkscrew?	**un sacacorchos?**	*oon sahkahkorchos*
a knife?	**un cuchillo?**	*oon koocheeyo*
a tin/can opener?	**un abrelatas?**	*oon ahbraylahtahs*
some cotton wool/balls?	**algodón?**	*ahlgodon*
some plasters/bandaids?	**tiritas?**	*teereetahs*
some rubbing alcohol?	**alcohol?**	*ahlkol*
some scissors?	**unas tijeras?**	*oonahs teehayrahs*
some soap?	**jabón?**	*hahbon*
some sunscreen?	**crema protectora?**	*kraymah protektorah*
some surgical tape?	**esparadrapo?**	*espahrahdrahpo*

Or if you're planning to hunt or fish ...

bait	**cebo** *(m.)*	*thaybo*
closed season	**veda** *(f.)*	*baydah*
fishing	**pesca** *(f.)*	*peskah*
fishing rod	**caña** *(f.)* **de pescar**	*kahnyah day peskahr*
hook	**anzuelo** *(m.)*	*ahnthwaylo*
hunting	**caza** *(f.)*	*kahthah*
hunting rifle	**escopeta** *(f.)*	*eskopaytah*
net	**red** *(f.)*	*rred*

And finally, some activities if you go to the mountains or the sea:

abseiling	**rápel** (m.)	**rrah**pel
canyoning	**barranquismo** (m.)	bahrrahn**kee**smo
climbing	**escalada** (f.)	eskah**lah**dah
diving	**submarinismo** (m.)	soobmahree**nee**smo
mountaineering	**alpinismo** (m.)	ahlpee**nee**smo
rafting	**rafting** (m.)	**rrahf**teen
snorkelling	**buceo** (m.)	boo**thay**o
surfing	**surf** (m.)	sorf
windsurfing	**windsurf** (m.)	**weend**sorf

At the pool or beach

How much does it cost to get into the swimming pool?
¿Cuánto cuesta la entrada a la piscina?
kwahnto **kwes**tah lah en**trah**dah ah lah pees**thee**nah

Is there a pool for kids?
¿Hay piscina para niños?
I pees**thee**nah **pah**rah **nee**nyos

Is it indoor?
¿Es cubierta?
es koo**byayr**tah

I'm looking for a ...	Busco una...	**boos**ko **oo**nah
beach with a lifeguard.	playa vigilada.	**plah**yah beehee**lah**dah
nude beach.	playa nudista.	**plah**yah noo**dee**stah

I would like to rent ...	Quisiera alquilar...	kee**syay**rah ahlkee**lahr**
a bathing/swim cap.	un gorro.	oon **gorr**o

a beach umbrella.	una sombrilla.	*oonah sombreeyah*
a diving mask.	gafas de buceo.	*gahfahs day boothayo*
flippers.	aletas.	*ahlaytahs*
a sunlounger.	una tumbona.	*oonah toombonah*
a towel.	una toalla.	*oonah toahyah*

What is the meaning of a flag that's ...?	¿Qué significa la bandera...	*kay seegneefeekah lah bahndayrah*
blue?	azul?	*ahthool*
green?	verde?	*bayrday*
yellow?	amarilla?	*ahmahreeya*
red?	roja?	*rrohah*

Camping

No ...	Está prohibido...	*estah proeebeedo*
camping on the beach.	acampar en la playa.	*ahkahmpahr en lah plahyah*
lighting fires in this area.	hacer fuego en esta zona.	*ahthayr fwaygo en estah thonah*

Does the campsite have ...	¿El camping tiene...	*el kahmpeen tyenay*
bungalows?	bungalows?	*boongahlos*
a laundry?	lavandería?	*lahbahndayreeah*
a parking area?	aparcamiento?	*ahpahrkahmyento*
a supermarket?	supermercado?	*soopayrmayrkahdo*

How much is it for ...	¿Cuál es la tarifa por...	*kwahl es lah tahreefah por*
one day?	día?	*deeah*
one week?	semana?	*saymahnah*

a camping car?	**autocaravana?**	*aootokahrah**bah**nah*
a caravan / trailer?	**caravana?**	*kahrah**bah**nah*
a tent?	**tienda de campaña?**	***tyen**dah day kahm**pah**nyah*

How much is ...	**¿Cuánto cuesta...**	***kwahn**to **kwes**tah*
a bungalow?	**un bungalow?**	*oon boongah**lo***
parking?	**el aparcamiento?**	*el ahpahrkah**myen**to*

How many does a bungalow sleep?
¿Cuántas personas caben en un bungalow?
kwahn**tahs payr**so**nahs **kah**ben en oon boongah**lo

Do the bungalows have individual showers?
¿Los bungalows tienen duchas individuales?
*los boongah**los tyen**en **doo**chahs eendeebee**dwah**lays*

Trees and plants

It is said that in Roman times, a squirrel could cross the Iberian Peninsula by jumping from tree to tree. Things have changed since then, but Spain remains heavily forested. To protect these wild areas, there are 14 **Parques Nacionales**: a permit must be obtained in advance in order to visit them.

How can we visit the Doñana National Park?
¿Cómo se puede visitar el Parque Nacional de Doñana?
***ko**mo say **pway**day beesee**tahr** el **pahr**kay nahthyo**nahl** day do**nyah**nah*

Do I need a permit to visit the Grazalema fir forest?
¿Necesito un permiso para visitar el pinsapar de Grazalema?
*naythay**see**to oon payr**mee**so **pah**rah beesee**tahr** el peensah**pahr** day grahthah**lay**mah*

Can you tell me ...	¿Puede decirme...	*pwayday daytheermay*
what is allowed?	**lo que está permitido?**	*lo kay estah paymeeteedo*
what is prohibited?	**lo que está prohibido?**	*lo kay estah proeebeedo*

Here are some trees and plants you might come across:

chestnut tree	**castaño** *(m.)*	*kahstahnyo*
fir tree	**abeto** *(m.)*	*ahbayto*
holm oak	**encina** *(f.)*	*entheenah*
oleander	**adelfa** *(f.)*	*ahdelfah*
olive tree	**olivo** *(m.)*	*oleebo*
palm tree	**palmera** *(f.)*	*pahlmayrah*
pine tree	**pino** *(m.)*	*peeno*

Animals

Spain has a large number of UNESCO-recognized **Reservas de la Biosfera** *Biosphere Reserves*, set up to protect biodiversity. Spain's three most threatened species are **el lince ibérico** *Iberian lynx*, **el oso pardo** *brown bear*, and **el águila imperial ibérica** *Spanish imperial eagle*. But Spain's most iconic animal is **el toro bravo** *fighting bull*. Whatever you may think of bullfighting, visiting **una ganadería** *breeding ranch* is a unique experience.

cat	**gato** *(m.)*	*gahto*
deer	**ciervo** *(m.)*	*thyayrbo*
dog	**perro** *(m.)*	*payrro*
donkey	**burro** *(m.)*	*boorro*
duck	**pato** *(m.)*	*pahto*
fox	**zorro** *(m.)*	*thorro*
frog	**rana** *(f.)*	*rrahnah*

hare	**liebre** (f.)	*l**yay**bray*
lizard	**lagarto** (m.)	*lah**gahr**to*
mouse	**ratón** (m.)	*rrah**ton***
partridge	**perdiz** (f.)	*payr**deeth***
quail	**codorniz** (f.)	*kodor**neeth***
rabbit	**conejo** (m.)	*ko**nay**ho*
rat	**rata** (f.)	***rrah**tah*
snake	**culebra** (f.)	*koo**lay**brah*
squirrel	**ardilla** (f.)	*ahr**dee**yah*
viper	**víbora** (f.)	***bee**borah*
wild boar	**jabalí** (m.)	*hahbah**lee***
wild game	**caza** (f.)	***kah**thah*
wolf	**lobo** (m.)	***lo**bo*

Bites, insects and allergies

Help! I've been stung by a scorpion!
¡Socorro! ¡Me ha picado un alacrán!
*so**ko**rro may ah pee**kah**do oon ahlah**krahn***

I need an antidote for a snakebite.
Necesito un antídoto contra las mordeduras de víbora.
*naythay**see**to oon ahn**tee**doto **kon**trah lahs morday**doo**rahs day **bee**borah*

I'd like some insect repellent.
Quisiera un repelente.
*kee**syay**rah oon rraypay**len**tay*

Insects and allergies

I'm allergic ... (m./f.)	Soy alérgico/-a...	*soy ah**layr**heeko/-ah*
to bees.	a las abejas.	*ah lahs ah**bay**hahs*
to mosquito bites.	a las picaduras de mosquito.	*ah lahs peekah**doo**rahs day mos**kee**to*

caterpillar	**oruga** *(f.)*	o**roo**gah
cockroach	**cucaracha** *(f.)*	kookah**rah**chah
fly	**mosca** *(f.)*	**mos**kah
mosquito	**mosquito** *(m.)*	mos**kee**to
mosquito net	**mosquitera** *(f.)*	moskee**tay**rah
scorpion	**alacrán** *(m.)*	ahlah**krahn**
spider	**araña** *(f.)*	ah**rah**nyah
tick	**garrapata** *(f.)*	gahrrah**pah**tah
wasp	**avispa** *(f.)*	ah**bee**spah

Effects and treatments

anti-inflammatory	**anti-inflamatorio** *(m.)*	**ahn**tee-eenflahmah**to**ryo
bite / sting	**picadura** *(f.)*	peekah**doo**rah
fluid retention / oedema	**edema** *(m.)*	ay**day**mah
injection / shot	**inyección** *(f.)*	eenyek**thyon**
insecticide	**insecticida** *(m.)*	eensektee**thee**dah
swollen	**inflamado**	eenflah**mah**do
syringe	**jeringuilla** *(f.)*	hayreen**ghee**yah
vaccine	**vacuna** *(f.)*	bah**koo**nah
venom	**veneno** *(m.)*	bay**nay**no

↗ Accommodation

Making a reservation

country cottage / inn	**casa** *(f.)* / **hotel** *(m.)* **rural**	**kah**sah / otel rro**orahl**
one/two/three-star hotel	**hotel** *(m.)* **de una / dos / tres estrellas**	otel day **oo**nah / dos / tres es**tray**yahs
youth hostel	**albergue** *(m.)* **de juventud**	ahl**bayr**gay day hoobentoo^d

I'd like ...	Quisiera...	keesyayrah
to reserve a room.	reservar una habitación.	rraysayrbahr oonah ahbeetahthyon
to make a reservation for two nights.	hacer una reserva para dos noches.	ahthayr oonah rraysayrbah pahrah dos nochays

I need ...	Necesitaría...	naythayseetahreeah
a single room.	una habitación individual.	oonah ahbeetahthyon eendeebeedwahl
a room with two beds.	una habitación con dos camas.	oonah ahbeetahthyon kon dos kahmahs
a room with a double bed.	una habitación con cama de matrimonio.	oonah ahbeetahthyon kon kahmah day mahtreemonyo
a double room with an extra bed.	una habitación doble con cama supletoria.	oonah ahbeetahthyon doblay kon kahmah sooplaytoryah

A deposit is required to hold the reservation.
Tiene que dejar una señal al hacer la reserva.
tyenay kay dayhahr oonah saynyahl ahl ahthayr lah rraysayrbah

Does the price include breakfast?
¿El precio incluye el desayuno?
el praythyo eenklooyay el daysahyoono

Do the rooms have air conditioning?
¿Hay aire acondicionado en las habitaciones?
I Iray ahkondeethyonahdo en lahs ahbeetahthyonays

Are animals allowed?
¿Se aceptan animales?
say ahtheptahn ahneemahlays

At the hotel

Do you have any rooms available?
¿Tiene habitaciones libres?
*tyenay ahbeetah**thyon**es **lee**brays*

For how many nights?
¿Para cuántas noches?
*pahrah **kwahn**tahs **no**chays*

Does it overlook the street or the courtyard?
¿Es exterior o interior?
*es ekstayr**yor** o eentayr**yor***

I'd like a room with a sea view.
Quisiera una habitación con vistas al mar.
*kee**syay**rah **oo**nah ahbeetah**thyon** kon **bee**stahs ahl mahr*

I've reserved a room in the name of …
He reservado una habitación a nombre de…
*ay rraysayr**bah**do **oo**nah ahbeetah**thyon** ah **nom**bray day*

Could you wake me tomorrow at six?
¿Podría despertarme mañana a las seis?
*po**dree**ah despayr**tahr**may mah**nyah**nah ah lahs **say**ees*

Do you have to dial a certain number to make an external call?
¿Hay que marcar algún número para llamar al exterior?
*I kay mahr**kahr** ahl**goon noo**mayro **pah**rah yah**mahr** ahl ekstayr**yor***

What time do we have to check out?
¿A qué hora tenemos que dejar la habitación?
*ah kay **o**rah tay**nay**mos kay day**hahr** lah ahbeetah**thyon***

Breakfast and services

Is there room service?
¿Hay servicio de habitaciones?
I sayr**bee**thyo day ahbeetah**thyon**ays

Do you have laundry service?
¿Tienen servicio de lavandería?
tyenen sayr**bee**thyo day lahbahnday**ree**ah

Spaniards tend to eat a simple breakfast, perhaps a pastry or
una tostada *toast* with butter, jam or **jamón serrano** *cured ham*,
washed down with a coffee or freshly squeezed orange juice.
Note that **un café** *a coffee* in Spain usually means an espresso –
if you want something bigger, you'll need to ask for a **café doble**
double or an **americano**, which has hot water added. If you have a
sweet tooth, you could try **churros**, cylindrical doughnuts coated
in sugar and served with hot chocolate.

Could I have ...	¿Me pone...	may **pon**ay
an espresso?	un café solo?	oon kah**fay** so**lo**
an espresso with a dash of milk?	un café cortado? un cortado?	oon kah**fay** kor**tah**do oon kor**tah**do
a double espresso with a lot of milk?	un café con leche?	oon kah**fay** kon **lay**chay
a glass of milk with a little coffee?	una manchada?	**oo**nah mahn**chah**dah
a decaf?	un descafeinado?	oon deskahfayee**nah**do
a tea (with milk)?	un té (con leche)?	oon tay kon **lay**chay
toast with butter?	una tostada de mantequilla?	**oo**nah tos**tah**dah day mahntay**kee**yah
toast with ham and tomato?	una tostada de jamón y tomate?	**oo**nah tos**tah**dah day hah**mon** ee to**mah**tay
toast with olive oil?	una tostada de aceite?	**oo**nah tos**tah**dah day ah**thay**eetay

Do you have ...	¿Tiene...	*tyen*ay
hot chocolate?	**chocolate?**	*choko**lah**tay*
churros?	**churros?**	*choo*rros
pastries?	**bollería / bollos?**	*boyay**reeah** / **bo**yos*
croissants?	**cruasanes?**	*krwah**sah**nays*
freshly squeezed orange juice?	**zumo de naranja natural?**	*thoomo day nah**rahn**hah nahtoo**rahl***

Resolving issues

The air conditioning ...	**El aire acondicionado...**	*el Iray ahkondeethyo**nah**do*
The heating ...	**La calefacción...**	*lah kahlayfahk**thyon***
The lift / elevator ...	**El ascensor ...**	*el ahsthen**sor***
The shower ...	**La ducha...**	*lah **doo**chah*
The telephone ...	**El teléfono...**	*el tay**lay**fono*
The television ...	**La tele...**	*lah **tay**lay*
... isn't working.	**...no funciona.**	*no foon**thyon**ah*

The sink / washbasin is blocked.
El lavabo está atascado.
*el lah**bah**bo es**tah** ahtahs**kah**do*

The faucet / tap is leaking.
El grifo gotea.
*el **gree**fo go**tay**ah*

A lightbulb has burned out.
Se ha fundido una bombilla.
*say ah foon**dee**do **oo**nah bom**bee**yah*

Checking out

We're ready to leave. Could we have the bill, please?
Ya nos vamos. ¿Me prepara la cuenta, por favor?
*yah nos **bah**mos may pray**pah**rah lah **kwen**tah por fah**bor***

Can I pay ...	¿Puedo pagarle...	*pway*do pah**gahr**lay
with a card?	con tarjeta?	kon tahr**hay**tah
in cash?	en efectivo / metálico?	en efek**tee**bo / may**tah**leeko

Do you need a receipt?
¿Necesita una factura?
nay**thay**see**tah oo**nah fahk**too**rah

↗ Eating and drinking

Because the early morning **el desayuno** *breakfast* is quite small, Spaniards will have a mid-morning snack, often at a café, so they can hold out until the main meal of the day: **la comida** *lunch*. This is usually eaten between 1 and 4 p.m. Later, a late-afternoon snack (**la merienda**) might be required, as most people eat their evening meal (**la cena** *dinner*) between 9 and 11.30 p.m. Friends might go out to a restaurant or meet up to make the rounds of their favourite tapas bars: **ir de tapeo**.

Going for tapas

In Spain, tapas are served in snack-sized portions, but you can also order larger sizes: **una media ración** ('a half portion') is double the size of a tapa, and **una ración** ('a portion') is double that, usually ordered to share between several people. **Pinchos**, or *pintxos* in Basque, are bar snacks that consist of a topping skewered to a small piece of bread with a toothpick.

Hello, can I have a draught beer?
Hola, ¿me pone una caña?
*o*lah may **po**nay **oo**nah **kah**nyah

What kind of tapas do you have?

¿Qué tapas tiene?

*kay **tah**pahs **tyen**ay*

I would like a tapa of ...	Póngame una tapa de...	**pon**gahmay **oo**nah **tah**pah day
anchovies. (cured)	anchoas.	ahn**cho**ahs
anchovies (fresh)	boquerones	bokay**ro**nays
... seasoned with garlic.	... adobados.	ahdo**bah**dos
... marinated.	... en vinagre.	en bee**nah**gray
bacon.	torreznos.	to**rrayth**nos
blood sausage.	morcilla.	mor**thee**yah
broad beans with ham.	habas con jamón.	**ah**bahs kon hah**mon**
cheese.	queso.	**kay**so
croquettes.	croquetas.	kro**kay**tahs
dried fruit / nuts.	frutos secos.	**froo**tos **say**kos
dried smoked meat.	cecina.	thay**thee**nah
dried tuna.	mojama.	mo**hah**mah
ham.	jamón.	hah**mon**
horse mackerel (grilled ~).	jureles a la plancha.	hoo**ray**lays ah lah **plahn**chah
kidneys in sherry.	riñones al jerez.	rree**nyo**nays ahl hay**reth**
meatballs.	albóndigas.	ahl**bon**deegahs
mushrooms (grilled ~).	champiñones a la plancha.	chahmpee**nyo**nays ah lah **plahn**chah
octopus (Galician style).	pulpo a la gallega.	**pool**po ah lah gah**yay**gah
olives (stuffed ~).	aceitunas rellenas.	ahthayee**too**nahs rray**yay**nahs
omelette with prawns.	tortita de camarones.	tor**tee**tah day kahmah**ro**nays
pork loin sandwich.	montadito de lomo.	montah**dee**to day **lo**mo
pork loin with tomato.	lomo con tomate.	**lo**mo kon to**mah**tay

potatoes	patatas	pahtahtahs
... with peppers.	... a lo pobre.	ah lo pobray
... with spicy sauce.	... a la brava.	ah lah brahbah
prawns	gambas	gahmbahs
... in batter.	... con gabardina.	kon gahbahrdeenah
... grilled.	... a la plancha.	ah lah plahnchah
... in garlic.	... al ajillo.	ahl ahheeyo
Russian salad.	ensaladilla rusa.	ensahlahdeeyah rroosah
seafood salad.	salpicón de marisco.	sahlpeekon day mahreesko
skewers of vegetables.	banderillas.	bahndayreeyahs
skewer of meat.	pincho moruno.	peencho moroono
Spanish omelette.	tortilla de patatas.	torteeyah day pahtahtahs
spinach with chickpeas.	espinacas con garbanzos.	espeenahkahs kon gahrbahnthos
squid (fried ~).	calamares fritos.	kahlahmahrays freetos
tripe.	callos.	kahyos

At the restaurant

I'd like to reserve a table for this evening.
Quisiera reservar una mesa para esta noche.
keesyayrah rraysayrbar oonah maysah pahrah estah nochay

At 10 o'clock, for four people, in the name of Pedro Angulo.
A las diez, para cuatro personas, a nombre de Pedro Angulo.
ah lahs dyeth pahrah kwahtro payrsonahs ah nombray day ...

Good evening, I reserved a table.
Buenas noches, he reservado una mesa.
bwaynahs nochays ay rraysayrbahdo oonah maysah

Would you happen to have a table for six people?
¿Tendría una mesa para seis personas?
tendreeah oonah maysah pahrah sayees payrsonahs

Have you reserved?
¿Tiene reserva?
tyenay rraysayrbah

I'm sorry, we are full.
Lo siento, estamos completos.
lo syento estahmos komplaytos

There's a 20-minute wait.
Hay veinte minutos de espera.
I bayeentay meenootos day espayrah

Many restaurants offer a fixed-price set of courses (**el menú**), which usually consists of **el primer plato** *first course*, **el segundo** *main course*, and **el postre** *dessert*. Almost always, **la bebida** *a drink* is included. Note that the word for *menu* is **la carta**. To ask for the bill, just say **La cuenta, por favor**. In terms of the tip (**la propina**), a service charge is included in the bill, so customers generally just leave 2 or 3 euros as a sign of appreciation, except in expensive restaurants.

Do you have a set menu?
¿Tienen menú?
tyenen maynoo

Will you bring me a menu, please?
¿Me trae la carta, por favor?
may trahay lah kahrtah por fahbor

Have you chosen?
¿Han elegido?
ahn aylayheedo

We're going to share the starters and then each have a main.
Vamos a compartir unos entrantes y luego cada uno tomará un plato.
bahmos ah kompahrteer oonos entrahntays ee lwaygo kahdah oono tomahrah oon plahto

I'll have the set menu. For the first course, I'll have … and then …
Voy a tomar un menú. De primero tomaré…, y de segundo…
boy ah tomahr oon maynoo day preemayro tomahray ee day saygoondo

What are you going to drink?
¿Qué van a beber?
kay bahn ah baybayr

I'd like fish: what do you recommend?
Quisiera algo de pescado: ¿qué me recomienda?
keesyayrah ahlgo day peskahdo kay may rraykomyendah

Do you prefer it fried or grilled?
¿Lo prefiere frito o a la plancha?
lo prayfyayray freeto o ah lah plahnchah

What does it come with?
¿Qué guarnición trae?
kay gwahrneethyon trahay

How do you like your meat cooked?
¿Cómo quiere la carne?
komo kyayray lah kahrnay

very rare	casi cruda	*kahsee **kroo**dah*
rare	poco hecha	*poko **ay**chah*
medium	al punto	*ahl **poon**to*
well done	muy hecha	*mooee **ay**chah*

Specialities and traditional dishes

Each region has its own specialities, with hearty soups and stews **platos de cuchara** ('dishes for the spoon') featuring heavily.

• **La paella** has its origins in a simple country dish from the region of Valencia. The authentic **paella valenciana** has rice, beans, vegetables, chicken, rabbit and snails. Today, seafood or mixed paella is the type that is best known internationally.
• **El cocido madrileño** is a chickpea-based stew with meat and vegetables from Madrid.
• **La fabada asturiana** is a meat and bean stew from Asturias.
• **El gazpacho andaluz** is a chilled soup from Andalusia made from tomatoes, peppers, cucumber and olive oil.
• **El lacón con grelos** is a Galician dish of pork shoulder with turnip greens.
• **El cochinillo asado** *roast suckling pig* from Segovia is so tender that it is sliced using the edge of a plate.

And if you still have room for dessert:
• **Los soplillos, buñuelos, rosquillas** are types of fritters or doughnuts that are typically eaten during Easter week.
• **El arroz con leche** *rice pudding* (made from milk, rice, sugar and vanilla) is served rather runny, with a stick of cinnamon.
• **La crema catalana** is the Spanish version of crème brûlée.
• **Las torrijas** is a Spanish version of French toast (eggy bread).
• **Las natillas** is a custard dessert.

Certain desserts are linked to religious festivals and are typically only found at that time of year. For the Christmas holidays, treats made from marzipan (**los mazapanes**) are very traditional, as well as shortbread made from flour, almonds and lard (**los mantecados**), and the similar but more crumbly **los polvorones**. Another Christmas speciality is **el turrón** *nougat*, hard or soft, made from honey, almonds, sugar and eggs. During the period of Epiphany in January (celebrating the visit of the Magi to the baby Jesus), you can find a special ring-shaped cake made from sweet brioche with candied fruit: **El Roscón de Reyes** ('Ring of Kings').

Food vocabulary

Here's some useful vocabulary if you go to **el mercado** *the market*.

Meat and poultry

Let's start at **la carnicería** *the butcher's*. (By the way, vegetarians should note that **la carne** refers to red meat – i.e. beef – so if you order a dish **sin carne** *without meat*, you might end up with poultry or ham! It's best just to say **Soy vegetariano/-a**.)

beef	**ternera** *(f.)*	*tayr**nay**rah*
breast	**pechuga** *(f.)*	*pay**choo**gah*
chicken	**pollo** *(m.)*	***po**yo*
ground beef	**carne** *(f.)* **picada**	***kahr**nay pee**kah**dah*
lamb chop	**chuletita** *(f.)* **de cordero**	*choolay**tee**tah day kor**day**ro*
pork chop	**chuleta** *(f.)* **de cerdo**	*choo**lay**tah day **thayr**do*
pork fat	**tocino** *(m.)*	*to**thee**no*
pork loin	**lomo** *(m.)* **de cerdo**	***lo**mo day **thayr**do*
rabbit	**conejo** *(m.)*	*ko**nay**ho*

steak (fillet)	**filete** *(m.)*	*fee**lay**tay*
steak (sirloin)	**solomillo** *(m.)* **de ternera**	*solo**mee**yo day tayr**nay**rah*
steak (T-bone)	**chuletón** *(m.)*	*choolay**ton***
thigh	**muslo** *(m.)*	***moos**lo*
turkey	**pavo** *(m.)*	***pah**bo*
veal	**ternera** *(f.)* **blanca**	*tayr**nay**rah **blahn**kah*
wing	**ala** *(m.)*	***ah**lah*

Cold cuts and offal

At the deli (**la charcutería**), you will find the celebrated **jamón ibérico pata negra**, cured ham from **el cerdo ibérico** *the Iberian pig*, which feeds on the acorns (**la bellota**) of oak forests. The counter that specializes in tripe and offal is called **la casquería**.

blood sausage	**morcilla** *(f.)*	*mor**thee**yah*
brains	**sesos** *(m.)*	***say**sos*
bull testicles	**criadillas** *(f.)*	*kryah**dee**yahs*
gizzard / sweetbreads	**molleja** *(f.)*	*mo**yay**hah*
ham	**jamón** *(m.)*	*hah**mon***
ham (boiled)	**jamón** *(m.)* **de york**	*hah**mon** day york*
ham (cured)	**jamón** *(m.)* **serrano / natural**	*hah**mon** sayr**rah**no / nahtoo**rahl***
ham (a slice)	**loncha** *(f.)* **de jamón**	***lon**chah day hah**mon***
heart	**corazón** *(m.)*	*korah**thon***
kidneys	**riñones** *(m.)*	*rree**nyo**nays*
liver	**hígado** *(m.)*	***ee**gahdo*
salami (cured sausage)	**salchichón** *(m.)*	*sahlchee**chon***
salami (a slice)	**rodaja** *(f.)* **de salchichón**	*rro**dah**hah day sahlchee**chon***
sausage	**salchicha** *(f.)*	*sahl**chee**chah*
tongue	**lengua** *(f.)*	***len**gwah*

Fish

The fish counter (**la pescadería**) in a Spanish market is a sight to behold – there is a huge variety of seafood (**el pescado** *fish* and **los mariscos** *shellfish*) in Spain.

Could I have three cuts of hake?
¿Me da tres rodajas de merluza?
*may dah tres rro**dah**hahs day mayr**loo**thah*

Could you clean the sea bream for me?
¿Me puede limpiar la dorada?
*may **pway**day leem**pyahr** lah do**rah**dah*

What fish do you recommend for pan frying?
Para frito, ¿qué me aconseja?
*pah*rah **free**to kay may ahkon**say**hah

anchovy (cured)	**anchoa** (f.)	ahn**cho**ah
anchovies (fresh)	**boquerones** (m.)	bokay**ro**nays
cockles	**berberechos** (m.)	bayrbay**ray**chos
cod (fresh)	**bacalao** (m.) **fresco**	bahkah**lao** fray**sko**
cod (salt)	**bacalao** (m.)	bahkah**lao**
cuttlefish	**sepia** (f.) / **jibia** (f.)	**say**pyah / **hee**byah
hake	**merluza** (f.)	mayr**loo**thah
lobster	**bogavante** (m.)	bogah**ban**tay
mackerel	**caballa** (f.)	kah**bah**yah
mussels	**mejillones** (m.)	mayhee**yo**nays
Norway lobster	**cigalas** (f. pl.)	thee**gah**lahs
octopus	**pulpo** (m.)	**pool**po
oysters	**ostras** (f.)	**o**strahs
prawns	**gambas** (f.)	**gahm**bahs

prawns (king)	**langostinos** (m.)	lahngo**stee**nos
red mullet	**salmonetes** (m. pl.)	sahlmo**nay**tays
salmon	**salmón** (m.)	sahl**mon**
sardines	**sardinas** (f.)	sahr**dee**nahs
sea bream	**dorada** (f.)	do**rah**dah
sole	**lenguado** (m.)	len**gwah**do
spiny lobster	**langosta** (f.)	lahn**go**stah
tuna	**atún** (m.)	ah**toon**
whiting	**pescadilla** (f.)	peskah**dee**yah

Fruits and vegetables

Finally, if you need **las frutas** *fruit* or **las verduras** *vegetables*, make a stop at **la verdulería** for produce.

almonds	**almendras** (f.)	ahl**men**drahs
apple	**manzana** (f.)	mahn**thah**nah
apricot	**albaricoque** (m.)	ahlbayree**ko**kay
artichoke	**alcachofa** (f.)	ahlkah**cho**fah
asparagus	**espárragos** (m. pl.)	es**pah**rrahgos
aubergine / eggplant	**berenjena** (f.)	bayren**hay**nah
avocado	**aguacate** (m.)	ahgwah**kah**tay
banana	**plátano** (m.)	**plah**tahno
beans (green / white)	**judías** (f.) **verdes** / **blancas**	hoo**dee**ahs **bayr**days / **blahn**kahs
blackberry	**mora** (f.)	**mo**rah
carrot	**zanahoria** (f.)	thahnah**o**ryah
cauliflower	**coliflor** (f.)	kolee**flor**
cherry	**cereza** (f.)	thay**ray**thah
chestnuts	**castañas** (f.)	kah**stah**nyahs
chickpeas	**garbanzos** (m.)	gahr**bahn**thos
coconut	**coco** (m.)	**ko**ko

courgette / zucchini	**calabacín** (m.)	kahlahbah**theen**
cucumber	**pepino** (m.)	pay**pee**no
fig	**higo** (m.)	**ee**go
garlic	**ajo** (m.)	**ah**ho
grape	**uva** (f.)	**oo**bah
grapefruit	**pomelo** (m.)	po**may**lo
hazelnuts	**avellanas** (f.)	ahbay**yah**nahs
leek	**puerro** (m.)	**pway**rro
legumes / pulses	**legumbres** (f.)	lay**goom**brays
lemon	**limón** (m.)	lee**mon**
lentils	**lentejas** (f.)	len**tay**hahs
lettuce	**lechuga** (f.)	lay**choo**gah
melon	**melón** (m.)	may**lon**
mushrooms	**champiñones** (m.)	chahmpee**nyo**nays
olives	**aceitunas** (f.)	ahthayee**too**nahs
onion	**cebolla** (f.)	thay**boy**ah
orange	**naranja** (f.)	nah**rahn**hah
parsley	**perejil** (m.)	payray**heel**
peach	**melocotón** (m.)	mayloko**ton**
pear	**pera** (f.)	**pay**rah
peas	**guisantes** (m.)	ghee**sahn**tays
pepper	**pimiento** (m.)	pee**myen**to
pineapple	**piña** (f.)	**pee**nya
plum	**ciruela** (f.)	theer**way**lah
potato	**patata** (f.)	pah**tah**tah
raisins	**pasas** (f.)	**pah**sahs
raspberry	**frambuesa** (f.)	frahm**bway**sah
strawberry	**fresa** (f.)	**fray**sah
tomato	**tomate** (m.)	to**mah**tay
vegetables (fresh)	**verduras** (f.)	bayr**doo**rahs
walnuts	**nueces** (f.)	**nway**thays
watermelon	**sandía** (f.)	san**dee**ah

Cooking methods and sauces

Preparation methods

An old saying has it that in northern Spain **se guisa** *it's stewed*, in central Spain **se asa** *it's roasted*, and in southern Spain **se fríe** *it's fried*, but in fact there are any number of ways of preparing food throughout the country.

• **a la plancha** *on a griddle* (for grilling meat, fish and vegetables without oil)
• **a la sal** *in a salt crust* (for roasting both fish and meat)
• **ahumado** *smoked* (for curing fish or meat)
• **al vapor** *steamed*
• **a la brasa** *barbecued*
• **hervido** *boiled*
• **asado** *roasted* or *baked*
• **marinado** *marinated*
• **adobado** marinated in vinegar, garlic, salt, oregano and **pimentón** *smoked paprika,* which gives **adobos** their red colour
• **en escabeche** marinated in an acidic mixture of oil, vinegar, white wine and spices.

Sauces

There are also a variety of **salsas** *sauces*:
• **la salsa romesco** is a Catalonian sauce made from tomatoes, garlic, almonds and **ñoras** *dried red peppers*.
• **el pil-pil** is a sauce that goes with **el bacalao** *salt cod* and **las gambas** *prawns*. It is made from olive oil, garlic and **la guindilla** *chili*, which are delicately stirred to create a spicy sauce.
• **el mojo picón** is a sauce from the Canary Islands that is prepared from garlic, **guindilla**, cumin, **pimentón**, vinegar, oil and salt ground together with a mortar and pestle.

Cheeses

Quesos *cheeses* come in three types: **de vaca** *from cow's milk*, **de cabra** *goat's milk*, or **de oveja** *sheep's milk*. In terms of aging, **queso fresco** is a creamy, unaged cheese, **tierno** is soft and mild; **semi-curado** is semi-aged, and **curado** is aged until it is hard and sharp. If you want an even riper cheese, try **queso viejo** ('old cheese').

The most well-known Spanish cheese is **queso manchego** ('cheese from La Mancha'), a pressed cheese made from sheep's milk, but there is great regional variety:
• **Queso de tetilla** ('nipple') from Galicia, named for its conical shape, is made from cow's milk. It is mild and creamy.
• **Torta del Casar** from Extremadura is a pressed cheese made from ewe's milk. It comes in a 7-cm-high wheel, from which the top of the rind is cut off to reach the creamy interior.
• **Cabrales** from Asturias is a blue cheese that you can identify by its strong smell, remembered long after tasting it!
• **Roncal** from Navarra is a hard, creamy sheep's milk cheese that becomes tangy with age.

Drinks

Spain is one of the world's largest wine producers, and its wines are exported far afield. **Rioja** and **Ribera del Duero** are the most well-known wine regions, but many others are today producing excellent **tinto** *red*, **blanco** *white* or **rosado** *rosé* wines.

Do you have a wine list?
¿Tiene carta de vinos?
tyenay kahrtah day beenos

Could you bring me ...	¿Me trae...	may **trahay**
a glass of ... ?	**una copa de... ?**	oonah **ko**pah day
a half a bottle of ... ?	**media botella de... ?**	**may**dyah bo**tay**yah day
a bottle of ... ?	**una botella de...?**	oonah bo**tay**yah day
a bottle of beer?	**una cerveza?**	oonah thayr**bay**thah

I'm going to have fish: what wine do you recommend?
Voy a comer pescado: ¿qué vino me recomienda?
*boy ah ko**mayr** pes**kah**do kay **bee**no may rrayko**myen**dah*

On the wine label, **la denominación de origen** *designation of origin* indicates where the wine was made. The number of years the wine has been aged is indicated by the categories **crianza** (at least 2 years for reds); **reserva** (at least 3 years for reds); **gran reserva** (at least 5 years for reds).

Apart from Spain's famous reds, you could try **Albariños** from Galicia, fruity white wines that pair well with seafood; or sherries from **Jerez**: the young **fino** and **manzanilla** sherries are dry and pale, while **amontillado** and **oloroso** are darker and nuttier. For a sweet dessert sherry, try **Pedro Ximénez**.

If you ask for **una cerveza** *a beer,* you may well get a bottle. For a draught beer, ask for **una caña**, about 20 cl (7 oz) although the size varies, **un tubo**, 25–33 cl (8–11 oz), or **una jarra** *mug* (a pint). A *shandy* (lager with lemon-lime soda) is **una clara**. After-dinner digestives and liqueurs (**licores**) are served in **un chupito** ('a little suck*') a shot*. There is **aguardiente** *eau-de-vie* or *schnapps*, **orujo** *grape-based pomace brandy*, **hierbas** liqueur made with a variety of plant aromas and herbs, and many more. Not to mention the mixed drinks:

• **La sangría:** red wine, sugar, lemon-lime soda and fruit

- **La queimada** (in Galicia): **orujo**, sugar, lemon peel, coffee and cinnamon, set alight and slowly burned
- **El rebujito** (in Sevilla): a dry manzanilla sherry spritzer with lemon-lime soda
- **El cubata:** any alcoholic drink with lemon-lime soda
- **El calimocho:** wine and Coca-Cola

For a drink without alcohol, ask for **una bebida sin alcohol**. **¡Salud!** *[sahloo^d]* Cheers!

Other beverages

Two Spanish specialities you might want to try are **la horchata**, a sweet drink that looks like milk but is made from crushed tiger nuts and is served ice-cold, and **los granizados**, sweetened fruit juices or cordials mixed into crushed ice. There are also coffee-based versions: **granizados de café**.

I'll have a/an ...	Voy a tomar un(a)...	boy ah to*mahr* oon/-ah
coffee with a shot of alcohol.	**carajillo.** *(m.)*	kahrah**hee**yo
coffee with sweetened condensed milk.	**bombón.** *(m.)*	bom**bon**
fruit juice. (fresh)	**zumo** *(m.)* **natural.**	**thoo**mo nahtoo**rahl**
herbal tea.	**infusión.** *(f.)*	eenfoo**syon**
hot chocolate.	**chocolate.** *(m.)*	choko**lahtay**
iced coffee.	**café** *(m.)* **con hielo.**	kah**fay** kon **yay**lo
milkshake.	**batido.** *(m.)*	bah**teedo**
soft drink.	**refresco.** *(m.)*	rray**fray**sko
tea.	**té.** *(m.)*	tay
water (mineral ~).	**agua** *(m.)* **mineral.**	**ah**gwah meenay**rahl**
water (sparkling ~).	**agua** *(m.)* **mineral con gas.**	**ah**gwah meenay**rahl** kon gahs
water (still mineral ~).	**agua** *(m.)* **mineral sin gas.**	**ah**gwah meenay**rahl** seen gahs

↗ Shopping

Shops and services

Aside from major shopping centres or districts, many shops are shut between 2 p.m. and 5 p.m. (and are closed on Sundays). However, shops stay open until at least 8 p.m. For food shopping, **el mercado** *the market* is the most traditional and vibrant place to go, and these are still found everywhere. You can always find a small local shop (**la tienda de barrio**) for basic provisions.

I'm looking for ...	Estoy buscando...	es**toy** boos**kahn**do
a bakery.	una panadería.	**oo**nah pahnahday**reeah**
a bank.	un banco.	oon **bahn**ko
a cake shop.	una pastelería.	**oo**nah pahstaylay**reeah**
a florist.	una floristería.	**oo**nah floreestay**reeah**
a greengrocer's / produce shop.	una verdulería. / una frutería.	**oo**nah bayrdoolay**reeah** / **oo**nah frootay**reeah**
a health food shop.	un herbolario.	oon ayrbo**lah**ryo
an ice cream shop.	una heladería.	**oo**nah aylahday**reeah**
a jeweller's.	una joyería.	**oo**nah hoyay**reeah**
a shoe-repairer/maker.	un zapatero.	oon thahpah**tay**ro
a shoe shop.	una zapatería.	**oo**nah thahpahtay**reeah**
a shop.	una tienda.	**oo**nah **tyen**dah
a shopping centre.	un centro comercial.	oon **then**tro komayr**thyahl**
a sports shop.	una tienda de deportes.	**oo**nah **tyen**dah day day**por**tays
a stand / kiosk.	un kiosco.	oon **kyos**ko
a tobacconist.	un estanco.	oon es**tahn**ko
a watchmaker's.	una relojería.	**oo**nah rraylohay**reeah**

If there's a line to be served at a market stand or at **la caja** *till/ checkout*, Spaniards will **pedir la vez** *ask who is last in the queue* (**la vez** is *one's turn in line*).

Who's the last in line?
¿Quién es el último?
kyen es el **ool**teemo

Who's before me?
¿Quién da la vez?
kyen dah lah beth

I'm (m./f.) the last in line.
Yo. Yo soy el último/la última.
yo yo soy el **ool**teemo / lah **ool**teemah

Other things you might hear or say in a shop

Are you being served?
¿Le atienden ya?
lay ah**tyen**den yah

What can I get for you?
¿Qué le pongo?
kay lay **pon**go

Is there a salesperson in the music section?
¿Hay algún dependiente en la sección de música?
I ahl**goon** daypen**dyen**tay en lah sek**thyon** day **moo**seekah

How much are the grapes?
¿Qué precio tienen las uvas? / ¿A cuánto están las uvas? /
¿A cómo están las uvas?
kay **pray**thyo **tyen**en lahs **oo**bahs / ah **kwahn**to es**tahn** lahs **oo**bahs /
ah **ko**mo es**tahn** lahs **oo**bahs

They're very reasonably priced.
Están muy bien de precio.
es**tahn** **moo**ee byen day **pray**thyo

They're a bit expensive.
Están un poco caras.
es**tahn** oon **po**ko **kah**rahs

Let me have a kilo. (NB: a kilogram is 2.2 pounds)
Póngame un kilo.
pongahmay oon **kee**lo

Anything else?
¿Algo más?
ahlgo mahs

Nothing else, thank you.
Nada más, gracias.
nahdah mahs **grah**thyahs

That will be 7 euros 80.
Son siete euros ochenta. / Son siete con ochenta.
son **syay**tay **ay**ooros o**chen**tah / son **syay**tay kon o**chen**tah

Here's your change.
Aquí tiene su vuelta.
ah**kee tyen**ay soo **bwel**tah

Books, newspapers, magazines and music

The main Spanish newspapers are **El País** (centre left), **El Mundo** and **ABC** (conservative), but the sports press has the most devoted readers: **Marca** and **As** (Real Madrid), **Sport** and **Mundo Deportivo** (F.C. Barcelona). If you're interested in music, note the difference between **una tienda de música**, which sells instruments, and **una tienda de discos**, which sells CDs, etc.

Excuse me, is there …	Disculpe, ¿hay…	dees**kool**pay I
a newspaper stand nearby?	un kiosco de periódicos en esta zona?	oon **kyos**ko day payree**o**deekos en **es**tah **tho**nah
a bookshop near here?	una librería por aquí?	**oo**nah leebray**ree**ah por ah**kee**
a CD shop not far away?	una tienda de discos no muy lejos?	**oo**nah **tyen**dah day **dees**kos no **mooee lay**hos

Do you have …	¿Tiene…	**tyen**ay
international papers?	prensa extranjera?	**pren**sah estrahn**hay**rah

newspapers in English?	periódicos en inglés?	payree**o**deekos en een**glays**
English / American / Canadian / Australian / New Zealand magazines?	revistas inglesas / americanas / canadienses / australianas / neozelandesas?	rray**bee**stahs een**glay**sahs / ahmayree**kah**nahs / kahnah**dyen**says / aoostrah**lyah**nahs / nayothaylahn**day**sahs
road maps?	mapas de carreteras?	**mah**pahs day kahrray**tay**rahs
tourist guidebooks?	guías turísticas?	**ghee**ahs too**rees**teekahs
comic books?	cómics? / tebeos?	**ko**meeks / tay**bay**os
language courses?	métodos de idioma?	**may**todos day ee**dyo**mah

Laundry and dry cleaning

Can you tell me where there is ...	¿Puede decirme dónde hay...	**pway**day day**theer**may **don**day I
a dry-cleaner's?	una tintorería?	**oo**nah teentoray**ree**ah
a launderette / laundromat?	una lavandería automática?	**oo**nah lahbanday**ree**ah aooto**mah**teekah

I'd like to leave these clothes with you.
Le dejo esta ropa.
lay **day**ho **es**tah **rro**pah

When will they be ready?
¿Para cuándo estará lista?
pahrah **kwan**do estah**rah** **lee**stah

Is it possible to have them ready a little earlier? I'm in a hurry.
¿No podría estar lista un poco antes? Me corre prisa.
no po**dree**ah es**tahr** **lee**stah oon **po**ko **ahn**tays may **ko**rray **pree**sah

They're clean; they just need ironing.
Está limpia, sería solo para un planchado.
estah leempyah sayreeah solo pahrah oon plahnchahdo

Shopping for clothes

Where is the ... department?	¿Dónde está la sección de...	donday estah lah sekthyon day
women's	señoras?	saynyorahs
children's clothes	ropa infantil?	rropah eenfahnteel
men's	caballeros?	kahbahyayros

Where are the dressing rooms?
¿Dónde están los probadores?
donday estahn los probahdorays

It's too big / small for me.
Me queda grande / pequeño.
may kaydah grahnday / paykaynyo

It's a bit short / a bit long.
Queda un poco corto / un poco largo.
kaydah oon poko korto / oon poko lahrgo

The sleeves are too long; they'll have to be shortened a few centimetres.
Las mangas me quedan muy largas, habría que meterles unos centímetros.
lahs mahngahs may kaydahn mooee lahrgahs ahbreeah kay maytayrlays oonos thenteemaytros

What size do you take? / What's your size?
¿Qué talla usa? / ¿Cuál es su talla?
kay tahyah oosah / kwahl es soo tahyah

I take a 42. (NB: Unfortunately, international clothes sizes vary! Some tags label the equivalent sizes in different countries.)
Gasto una cuarenta y dos.
gahsto oonah kwahrentah ee dos

Do you do alterations?
¿Hacen ustedes los arreglos?
ahthen oostaydays los ahrrayglos

They're / It's too tight.
Me aprieta. (shoes)
may ahpryaytah
Me queda muy estrecho/-a. (clothes)
may kaydah mooee estraycho/-ah

It's too big.
Es demasiado ancho.
es daymahsyahdo ahncho

They hurt.
Me hacen daño. (shoes)
may ahthen dahnyo

It fits well. / It suits me.
Me queda bien.
may kaydah byen

It doesn't fit / suit me at all.
Me queda fatal.
may kaydah fahtahl

And some vocabulary for clothing and accessories:

belt	**cinturón** *(m.)*	*theentoo**ron***
blouse	**blusa** *(f.)*	***bloo**sah*
boots	**botas** *(f.)*	***bo**tahs*
bra	**sujetador** *(m.)*	*soohaytah**dor***
cap (baseball)	**gorra** *(f.)*	***go**rrah*
coat / overcoat	**abrigo** *(m.)*	*ah**bree**go*
corduroy	**pana** *(f.)*	***pah**nah*
dress	**vestido** *(m.)*	*bes**tee**do*
espadrilles	**alpargatas** *(f.)*	*ahlpahr**gah**tahs*
gabardine	**gabardina** *(f.)*	*gahbahr**dee**nah*
gloves	**guantes** *(m.)*	***gwahn**tays*
hat (knitted)	**gorro** *(m.)*	***go**rro*
hat (with brim)	**sombrero** *(m.)*	*som**bray**ro*
jacket (leather/denim)	**cazadora** *(f.)*	*kahthah**do**rah*
jacket (sports coat)	**chaqueta** *(f.)* / **americana** *(f.)*	*chah**kay**tah / ahmayree**kah**nah*
jeans	**vaqueros** *(m.)*	*bah**kay**rros*
jumper / sweater	**jersey** *(m.)*	*hayr**say***
knickers / panties	**bragas** *(f.)*	***brah**gahs*
nightgown	**camisón** *(m.)*	*kahmee**son***
pantyhose / tights	**panty** *(m.)*	***pahn**tee*
sandals	**sandalias** *(f.)*	*sahn**dahl**yahs*
scarf	**bufanda** *(f.)*	*boo**fahn**dah*
shoes	**zapatos** *(m.)*	*thah**pah**tos*
… with laces	**… con cordones / abotinados**	*kon kor**do**nays ahboteen**ah**dos*
… with heels	**… de tacón**	*day tah**kon***
…for the beach	**… de playa**	*day **plah**yah*
… dress shoes	**… de vestir**	*day bes**teer***
… sports shoes	**… deportivos**	*daypor**tee**bos*

... leather shoes	... de cuero	day **kway**ro
... flats	... de tapa plana	day **tahpah plah**nah
shirt	**camisa** (f.)	kah**mee**sah
... short-sleeved	... de manga corta	day **mahn**gah **kor**tah
... striped	... de rayas	day **rrah**yahs
... patterned	... estampada	estahm**pah**dah
... solid-coloured	... lisa	**lee**sah
shorts	**pantalón** (m.) **corto**	pahntah**lon kor**to
skirt	**falda** (f.)	**fahl**dah
socks	**calcetines** (m.)	kahlthay**tee**nays
stockings / tights	**medias** (f.)	**may**dyahs
suit	**traje** (m.)	**trah**hay
swimsuit	**bañador** (m.)	bahnyah**dor**
T-shirt	**camiseta** (f.)	kahmee**say**tah
tie	**corbata** (f.)	kor**bah**tah
tracksuit	**chándal** (m.)	**chan**dahl
trainers / tennis shoes	**deportivas** (m.)	daypor**tee**bahs
trousers	**pantalón** (m.)	pahntah**lon**
... for winter	... de invierno	day een**byayr**no
... for summer	... de verano	day bay**rah**no
... for mid-season	... de entretiempo	day entray**tyem**po
... cotton	... de algodón	day ahlgo**don**
... flannel	... de franela	day frah**nay**lah
... woollen	... de lana	day **lah**nah
... tight	... ceñido	thay**nyee**do
underpants (men's)	**calzoncillo** (m.)	kahlthon**thee**yo
underwear	**ropa** (f.) **interior**	**rro**pah eentayr**yor**
waistcoat / vest	**chaleco** (m.)	chah**lay**ko

If you need to ask for a colour: **negro** black, **marrón** brown, **azul** blue, **verde** green, **púrpura** purple, **rojo** red, **rosa** pink, **blanco** white, **amarillo** yellow and **naranja** orange.

Smoking

Smoking is prohibited in indoor public spaces. However, you can smoke at the outdoor tables of street cafés. **El estanco** *the tobacconist* will have everything you need. Tobacco shops can be identified by the brown and yellow 'T' sign. If you need *an ashtray*, ask for **un cenicero**.

I'd like ...	Quisiera...	kee**syay**rah
a packet of cigarettes.	un paquete de cigarrillos.	oon pah**kay**tay day theega**ree**yos
a carton of ...	un cartón de...	oon kahr**ton** day
a cigar.	un puro.	oon **poo**ro
a box of cigars.	una caja de puros.	oonah **kah**hah day **poo**ros
pipe tobacco.	tabaco de pipa.	tah**bah**ko day **pee**pah
rolling tobacco.	tabaco de liar.	tah**bah**ko day lyahr
rolling paper.	papel de liar.	pah**pel** day lyahr
a box of matches.	una caja de cerillas.	oonah **kah**hah day thay**ree**yahs
a lighter.	un mechero.	oon may**chay**ro

At the photo shop

I'd like ...	Quisiera...	kee**syay**rah
to have these photos printed.	sacar unas copias de estas fotos en papel.	sah**kahr** oonahs **ko**pyahs day **es**tahs **fo**tos en pah**pel**
a 4 GB memory card.	una tarjeta de 4 gigas.	oonah tahr**hay**tah day **kwah**tro **hee**gahs
batteries.	pilas.	**pee**lahs
rechargeable batteries.	pilas recargables.	**pee**lahs rraykahr**gah**blays

Do you develop photos?
¿Hacen revelados?
ahthen rrraybay**lah**dos

I'd like them developed on glossy / matte / semi-gloss paper.
Quisiera un revelado en papel brillo, mate, semi mate.
kee**syay**rah oon rrraybay**lah**do en pah**pel bree**yo **mah**tay **say**mee **mah**tay

camera	**cámara** (f.)	**kah**mahrah
lens	**objetivo** (m.) / **lente** (m.)	obhay**tee**bo / **len**tay
... wide angle	**...gran angular**	grahn ahngoo**lahr**
tripod	**trípode** (m.)	**tree**poday
video camera	**videocámara** (f.)	beedayo**kah**mahrah

My camera's not working properly.
Se me ha estropeado la cámara.
say may ah estropay**ah**do lah **kah**mahrah

It's not focusing well.
No enfoca bien.
no en**fo**kah byen

Provisions and toiletries

biscuits / cookies	**galletas** (f.)	gah**yay**tahs
bread	**pan** (m.)	pahn
... sliced	**... de molde**	day **mol**day
bread (baguette)	**barra** (f.)	**bah**rrah
butter	**mantequilla** (f.)	mahntay**kee**yah
comb	**peine** (m.)	**pay**eenay

deodorant	**desodorante** (m.)	desodo**rahn**tay
eggs	**huevos** (m.)	**way**bos
flour	**harina** (f.)	ah**ree**nah
glass (drinking)	**vaso** (m.)	**bah**so
ice cream	**helado** (m.)	ay**lah**do
ice cubes	**cubitos** (m.) **de hielo**	koo**bee**tos day **yay**lo
jam	**mermelada** (f.)	mayrmay**lah**dah
knife	**cuchillo** (m.)	koo**chee**yo
lipstick	**barra** (f.) **de labios**	**bah**rrah day **lah**byos
mascara	**rímel** (m.)	**rree**mel
milk	**leche** (f.)	**lay**chay
mustard	**mostaza** (f.)	mo**stah**thah
oil	**aceite** (m.)	ah**thay**eetay
olives	**aceitunas** (f.)	ahthayee**too**nahs
pasta	**pasta** (f.)	**pah**stah
pepper	**pimienta** (f.)	pee**myen**tah
perfume	**perfume** (m.)	payr**foo**may
razor blades	**cuchillas** (f.) **de afeitar**	koo**chee**yahs day ahfayee**tahr**
rice	**arroz** (m.)	ah**rroth**
salt	**sal** (f.)	sahl
sandwich	**bocadillo** (m.) (baguette)	bokah**dee**yo
	sándwich (m.) (sliced bread)	**san**weech
serviette / napkin	**servilleta** (f.)	sayr**byay**tah
shampoo	**champú** (m.)	chahm**poo**
soap	**jabón** (m.)	hah**bon**
sugar	**azúcar** (m.)	ah**thoo**kahr
sweets / candies	**caramelos** (m.) / **chuches** (m.)	kahrah**may**los / **choo**chays
tin can	**lata** (f.)	**lah**tah

tissue / kleenex	**pañuelo** *(m.)*	*pahn**way**lo*
toilet paper	**papel** *(m.)* **higiénico**	*pah**pel** eeheeayneeko*
toothbrush	**cepillo** *(m.)* **de dientes**	*thay**pee**yo day **dyen**tays*
toothpaste	**pasta** *(f.)* **de dientes**	***pah**stah day **dyen**tays*
vinegar	**vinagre** *(m.)*	*beenah**gray***
wine	**vino** *(m.)*	***bee**no*

Souvenirs

There is no shortage of choice of presents to take back home. Many shops sell delectable traditional foods; you can even get **jamón ibérico** vacuum-packed to travel. There are also typical local crafts, from **los cuchillos** *knives* (especially from Toledo and Albacete) to **la alfarería** *pottery*, or **los abanicos** *fans*, some of which are beautifully handcrafted.

Spain is also famous for its high-quality handcrafted leather goods (**marroquinería**), including coats, jackets, bags, shoes and gloves. A traditional leather wineskin flask is **una bota**. A Spanish shawl (**una mantilla**) is also a popular gift idea.

I'd like to take back a souvenir from Spain for friends; what do you recommend?
Quisiera llevarles un recuerdo de España a unos amigos, ¿qué me aconsejaría?
*kee**syay**rah yay**bahr**lays oon rray**kwayr**do day es**pah**nyah ah **oo**nos ah**mee**gos kay may ahkonsayhah**reeah***

It's a gift; could you wrap it for me?
Es para regalo, ¿me lo podría envolver?
*es **pah**rah rray**gah**lo may lo po**dree**ah enbol**bayr***

↗ Business meetings

If you're in Spain for business, here is some useful vocabulary to help you get by **en la oficina** in the office.

Making an appointment

I'd like an appointment with Mr Hernandez.
Quisiera una cita con el señor Hernández.
*kee**syay**rah **oo**nah **thee**tah kon el say**nyor** ayr**nahn**deth*

Could you make me an appointment with Ms Salvatierra?
¿Me puede dar una cita con la señora Salvatierra?
*may **pway**day dahr **oo**nah **thee**tah kon lah say**nyo**rah sahlbah**tyay**rrah*

Or if you don't have the name of a specific person:

the person in charge of marketing (m./f.)	el / la responsable de marketing	el / lah rrayspon**sah**blay day **mahr**kayteen
the person in charge of accounts (m./f.)	el / la responsable de contabilidad	el / lah rrayspon**sah**blay day kontahbeelee**da**d
the director of human resources (m./f.)	el director / la directora de recursos humanos	el deerek**tor** / lah deerek**tor**ah day rray**koor**sos oo**mah**nos
the head of maintenance (m./f.)	el jefe / la jefa de mantenimiento	el **hay**fay / lah **hay**fah day mahntenee**myen**to
the managing director (m./f.)	el consejero delegado / la consejera delegada	el / lah konsay**hay**ro/-ah daylay**gah**do/-ah

Tuesday at 5:00 p.m., is that convenient for you?
El martes a las cinco, ¿le viene bien?
*el **mahr**tays ah lahs **theen**ko lay **byen**ay byen*

Perfect, let's arrange it for then!
Perfecto, ¡pues quedamos en eso!
*payr**fek**to pways kay**dah**mos en **ay**so*

In the workplace

branch / subsidiary	filial (f.)	feelyahl
chain	cadena (f.)	kahdaynah
company	empresa (f.)	empraysah
factory	fábrica (f.)	fahbreekah
franchise	franquicia (f.)	frahnkeethyah
hangar	nave (f.)	nahbay
head	jefe / jefa (m./f.)	hayfay / hayfah
headquarters	sede (f.)	sayday
intern / trainee	becario/-a (m./f.)	baykahryo/-ah
manager	ejecutivo/-a (m./f.)	ayhaykooteebo/-ah
office	oficina (f.)	ofeetheenah
plant	planta (f.)	plahntah
research and development	investigación (f.) y desarrollo (m.)	eenbesteegahthyon ee desahrroyo
SME (small and medium-sized company)	PYME (f.) (pequeña y mediana empresa)	peemay paykaynyah ee maydyahnah empraysah
staff / personnel	plantilla (f.)	plahnteeyah
stock / supply	existencias (f.)	ekseestenthyahs
storage	almacenamiento (m.)	ahlmahthaynahmyento
temporary worker	interino/-a (m./f.)	eentayreeno/-ah
warehouse	almacén (m.)	ahlmahthen
worker	obrero/-a / operario/-a (m./f.)	obrayro/-ah / opayrahryo/-ah
workshop	taller (m.)	tahyayr

Business vocabulary

amount	importe (m.)	eemportay
apprenticeship	aprendizaje (m.)	ahprendeethahhay
balance (remainder)	saldo (m.)	sahldo

balance sheet	**balance** *(m.)*	bah**lahn**thay
budget	**presupuesto** *(m.)*	praysoo**pwes**to
buyer	**comprador** *(m.)*	komprah**dor**
cash flow	**caja** *(f.)*	**kah**hah
competition	**competencia** *(f.)*	kompay**ten**thyah
consulting firm	**asesoría** *(f.)*	ahsayso**ree**ah
cost	**coste** *(m.)*	**kos**tay
credit an account	**abonar en cuenta**	ahbo**nahr** en **kwen**tah
debit an account	**cargar en cuenta**	kahr**gahr** en **kwen**tah
headhunter	**cazatalentos** *(m./f.)*	kahthahtah**len**tos
hire (to ~)	**contratar**	kontrah**tahr**
investment	**inversion** *(f.)*	eenbayr**syon**
investor	**inversor** *(m.)*	eenbayr**sor**
lay off (to ~)	**despedir**	despay**deer**
loan	**préstamo** *(m.)*	**pray**stahmo
market share	**cuota** *(f.)* **de mercado**	**kwo**tah day mayr**kah**do
order	**pedido** *(m.)*	pay**dee**do
overtime	**horas** *(f.)* **extra(s)**	**o**rahs **es**trah(s)
patent	**patente** *(f.)*	pah**ten**tay
pay in (to ~)	**cobrar**	ko**brahr**
payment	**pago** *(m.)*	**pah**go
payslip	**nómina** *(f.)*	**no**meenah
purchase	**compra** *(f.)*	**kom**prah
retailer	**minorista** *(m./f.)*	meeno**ree**stah
retirement	**jubilación** *(f.)*	hoobeelah**thyon**
shareholder	**accionista** *(m./f.)*	ahkthyo**nee**stah
sign (to ~)	**firmar**	feer**mahr**
sponsor	**patrocinador/a** *(m./f.)*	pahtrotheenah**dor**/-ah
sub-contractor	**subcontratista** *(m./f.)*	soobkontrah**tee**stah
supplier	**proveedor/a** *(m./f.)*	probayay**dor**/-ah

turnover	**facturación** (f.) / **volumen** (m.) de **negocios**	*fahktoorah***thyon** / *bo***loo***men day naygothyos*
unemployment	**paro** (m.) / **desempleo** (m.)	**pah**ro / *desem***play**o
unpaid	**impago** (m.)	*eem***pah**go
wholesaler	**mayorista** (m./f.)	*mahyo***ree**stah

Fairs and trade shows

The **IFEMA (Institución Ferial de Madrid)** is one of the largest spaces for trade shows in Europe. The famous **FITUR (Feria Internacional del Turismo)** tourism fair is held there every year. An exhibitor at a fair is **un expositor**.

aisle	**pasillo** (m.)	*pah***see**yo
exhibition ground	**recinto ferial** (m.)	*rray***theen**to *fayree***ahl**
fair	**feria** (f.)	**fay**reeah
hall	**pabellón** (m.)	*pahbay***yon**
new product	**novedad** (f.)	*nobay***da**^{d}
product range	**oferta** (f.)	*o***fayr**tah
request	**demanda** (f.)	*day***mahn**dah
sample	**muestra** (f.)	**mway**strah
stand / stall	**stand** (m.)	*es***tan**^{d}
trade fair / show	**salón** (m.)	*sah***lon**

↗ Health

If you need medical attention ...

Residents of the European Union can request a *European Health Insurance Card* (EHIC) before travelling to another European country. This allows access to free or reduced-cost state-provided health care if you fall ill or have an accident. Non-EU visitors should make sure they have insurance. Primary care is provided at local **centros de salud** *health centres*, but if specialist or emergency care is required, this may involve a hospital.

Where is the nearest health centre?
¿Dónde está el centro de salud más cercano?
*don*day es*tah* el *then*tro day sah*loo*ᵈ mahs thayr*kah*no

I need to go to the emergency room. Where is the hospital?
Necesito ir a urgencias. ¿Dónde está el hospital?
naythay*see*to eer ah oor*hen*thyahs *don*day es*tah* el ospee*tahl*

This is my European Health Insurance Card.
Esta es mi tarjeta sanitaria europea.
*es*tah es mee tahr*hay*tah sahnee*tahr*yah ayooro*pay*ah

I have a temperature. Could I see a doctor?
Estoy con fiebre. ¿Me podría ver un médico?
es*toy* kon *fye*bray may po*dree*ah bayr oon *may*deeko

When will he/she be able to see me?
¿Cuándo me podrá atender?
*kwahn*do may po*drah* ahten*dayr*

Symptoms

I don't feel well.
No me encuentro bien.
no may en*kwen*tro byen

I am ... (m./f.)	Estoy...	estoy
ill.	enfermo/-a.	enfayrmo/-ah
congested. / I have a cold.	constipado/-a. acatarrado/-a. resfriado/-a.	konsteepahdo/-ah ahkahtahrrahdo/-ah rresfreeahdo/-ah
constipated.	estreñido/-a.	estraynyeedo/-ah

I fainted.
Me he desmayado.
may ay desmahyahdo

I'm dizzy. (m./f.)
Estoy mareado/-a.
estoy mahrayahdo/-ah

I've been vomiting.
Tengo vómitos.
tengo bomeetos

I'm having difficulty breathing.
Me cuesta trabajo respirar.
may kwestah trahbahho rrespeerahr

I'm coughing a lot.
Tengo mucha tos.
tengo moochah tos

I have chills.
Siento escalofríos.
syento eskahlofreeos

I think I have high / low blood pressure.
Creo que tengo la tensión alta / baja.
krayo kay tengo lah tensyon ahltah/bahhah

Pains and body parts

My ... hurts.	Me duele...	may dwaylay
ankle	el tobillo.	el tobeeyo
arm	el brazo.	el brahtho
back	la espalda.	lah espahldah
chest	el pecho.	el paycho
foot	el pie.	el pyay

head	la cabeza.	lah kah**bay**thah
knee	la rodilla.	lah rro**dee**yah
leg	la pierna.	lah **pyayr**nah
liver	el hígado.	el **ee**gahdo
neck	el cuello.	el **kway**yo
shoulder	el hombro.	el **om**bro
stomach	el estómago.	el es**to**mahgo
throat	la garganta.	lah gahr**gahn**tah

My ... hurt.	Me duelen...	may **dway**len
ears	los oídos.	los o**ee**dos
joints	las articulaciones.	lahs ahrteekoolah**thyon**ays
kidneys	los riñones.	los rree**nyo**nays

I am ... (m./f.)	Soy...	soy
allergic.	alérgico/-a.	ah**layr**heeko/-ah
asthmatic.	asmático/-a.	ahs**mah**teeko/-ah
diabetic.	diabético/-a.	dyah**bay**teeko/-ah
epileptic.	epiléptico/-a.	epee**lep**teeko/-ah

I have a heart problem.
Tengo un problema de corazón.
*ten*go oon pro**blay**mah day korah**thon**

I've burned myself.
Me he quemado.
*may ay kay**mah**do*

I've cut myself.
Me he cortado.
*may ay kor**tah**do*

I have broken my ...	Me he roto...	may ay **rro**to
arm.	un brazo.	oon **brah**tho

finger.	un dedo.	oon **day**do
hand.	la mano.	lah **ma**no
leg.	la pierna.	lah **pyayr**nah
nose.	la nariz.	lah nah**reeth**
wrist.	la muñeca.	lah moon**yay**kah
a bone in my foot.	un hueso del pie.	oon **way**so del pyay

I feel stiff.
Tengo agujetas.

*ten*go ahgoo**hay**tahs

I have a cramp.
Me ha dado un calambre.

*may ah **dah**do oon kah**lahm**bray*

Women's health

abort (to ~)	abortar	ahbor**tahr**
abortion	aborto (m.)	ah**bor**to
birth (to give ~)	dar a luz	dahr ah looth
contraceptive	anticonceptivo (m.)	ahnteekonthep**tee**bo
cystitis	cystitis (f.)	thee**stee**tees
diaphragm	diafragma (m.)	dyah**frag**mah
labour / childbirth	parto (m.)	**pahr**to
period	regla (f.)	**rray**glah
pill (morning-after)	píldora (f.) (del día después)	**peel**dorah del **dee**ah des**pways**
pregnancy	embarazo (m.)	embah**rah**tho
tampons	tampones (m.)	tahm**po**nays

I'm having my period. Do you have tablets for the pain?
Estoy con la regla. ¿Tiene alguna pastilla para el dolor?

es**toy** kon lah **rray**glah **tye**nay ahl**goo**nah pah**stee**yah **pah**rah el do**lor**

I'm two months late.
Tengo un retraso de dos meses.

*ten*go oon rray**trah**so day dos **may**says

I'm pregnant.
Estoy embarazada.
estoy embahrahthahdah

I'm six months pregnant.
Estoy de seis meses.
estoy day sayees maysays

Getting treatment

Don't worry.
No se preocupe.
no say prayokoopay

It's nothing serious.
No es nada grave.
no es nahdah grahbay

We'll have to put a cast on.
Hay que poner una escayola.
I kay ponayr oonah eskahyolah

We need to do ...	Hay que hacer...	I kay ahthayr
some examinations.	unas pruebas.	oonahs prwaybahs
some tests.	unos análisis.	oonos ahnahleesees
an X-ray.	una radiografía.	oonah rrahdyograhfeeah

I'm going to ...	Voy a...	boy ah
prescribe you some medication.	recetarle unas medicinas.	rraythaytahrlay oonahs maydeetheenahs
send you to a specialist.	dirigirle a un especialista.	deereeheerlay ah oon espaythyahleestah
examine you.	reconocerlo/-a.	rraykonothayrlo/-ah

You will need to ...	Va a tener que...	bah ah taynayr kay
stay in bed.	guardar cama.	gwahrdahr kahmah
get injections.	ponerse unas inyecciones.	ponayrsay oonahs eenyekthyonays
follow aftercare treatment instructions.	hacerse unas curas.	ahthayrsay oonahs koorahs

take a mixture / syrup.	tomarse un jarabe.	to**mahr**say oon hah**rah**bay
take some tablets.	tomarse unas pastillas.	to**mahr**say **oo**nahs pah**stee**yahs
have an operation.	operarse.	opay**rahr**say

At the dentist's

I have a toothache.	Me duelen las muelas.	may **dway**len lahs **mway**lahs
I have an abscess.	Tengo un flemón.	**ten**go oon flay**mon**
I have a cavity.	Tengo una muela picada.	**ten**go **oo**nah **mway**lah pee**kah**dah
I've lost a filling.	Se me ha caído un empaste.	say may ah ka**hee**do oon em**pah**stay

I'm going to have to ...	Voy a tener que...	boy ah tay**nayr** kay
pull out a tooth.	sacarle una muela.	sah**kahr**lay **oo**nah **mway**lah
give you a filling.	hacerle un empaste.	ah**thayr**lay oon em**pah**stay
deaden the nerve.	matarle el nervio.	mah**tahr**lay el **nayr**byo
give you a root canal.	hacerle una endodoncia.	ah**thayr**lay **oo**nah endo**don**thyah

Open your mouth.	¡Abra la boca!	**ah**brah lah **bo**kah
Rinse your mouth.	¡Enjuáguese la boca!	en**hwah**gaysay lah **bo**kah
Spit.	¡Escupa!	es**koo**pah

At the optician's

I've broken my glasses.
Se me han roto las gafas.
say may ahn **rro**to lahs **gah**fahs

I've broken a lens.
Se me ha roto un cristal.
say may ah **rro**to oon kree**stahl**

I need ...	Necesitaría...	naythayseetahreeah
a pair of sunglasses.	unas gafas de sol.	oonahs gahfahs day sol
contact lenses.	lentillas.	lenteeyahs

Could you ...	¿Podría...	podreeah
check my vision?	graduarme la vista?	grahdwahrmay lah beestah
show me some frames?	enseñarme unas monturas?	ensaynyahrmay oonahs montoorahs

At the pharmacy

La farmacia *chemist's, drugstore* can be spotted by a neon green cross, which is lit up when open.

Can you tell me where I can find a pharmacy?
¿Puede indicarme dónde hay una farmacia?
pwayday eendeekahrmay donday I oonah fahrmahthyah

This is my prescription.
Traigo esta receta.
trIgo estah rraythaytah

Could you give me something for ...	¿Podría darme algo para...	podreeah dahrmay ahlgo pahrah
burns?	las quemaduras?	lahs kaymahdoorahs
a cold?	el resfriado?	el rresfreeahdo
a cough?	la tos?	lah tos
diarrhoea?	la diarrea?	lah dyahrrayah
a sore throat?	la garganta?	lah gahrgahntah
a stomachache?	el dolor de estómago?	el dolor day estomahgo
a toothache?	el dolor de muelas?	el dolor day mwaylahs

I'd like ...	Quisiera...	kee*syay*rah
an antiseptic.	un antiséptico.	oon ahntee*sep*teeko
some aspirin.	aspirina.	ahspee*ree*nah
a pain reliever.	un analgésico.	oon ahnahl*hay*seeko
something for a fever.	un antitérmico.	oon ahntee*tayr*meeko
cotton pads.	algodón.	ahlgo*don*
plasters / bandaids.	tiritas.	tee*ree*tahs
sun cream / sunscreen.	protector solar.	protek*tor* so*lahr*
surgical tape.	esparadrapo.	espahrah*drah*po

Index